The Roaring Girl

THE NEW MERMAIDS

General Editor: Brian Gibbons
Professor of English Literature, University of Münster

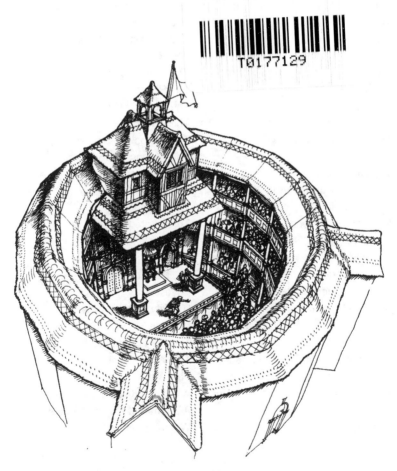

Reconstruction of an Elizabethan theatre by C. Walter Hodges

THE NEW MERMAIDS

The Roaring Girl

THOMAS MIDDLETON
AND THOMAS DEKKER

Edited by
ELIZABETH COOK

B L O O M S B U R Y
LONDON • NEW DELHI • NEW YORK • SYDNEY

Bloomsbury Methuen Drama
An imprint of Bloomsbury Publishing Plc

50 Bedford Square
London
WC1B 3DP
UK

1385 Broadway
New York
NY 10018
USA

www.bloomsbury.com

Bloomsbury is a registered trade mark of Bloomsbury Publishing Plc

Second Edition 1997
Published by A & C Black Publishers Limited

© 1997 A & C Black Publishers Limited

First New Mermaid edition 1976
Ernest Benn Limited

© 1976 by Ernest Benn Limited

Visit www.bloomsbury.com to find out more about our authors and their books
You will find extracts, author interviews, author events and you can sign up for
newsletters to be the first to hear about our latest releases and special offers.

British Library Cataloguing-in-Publication Data
A catalogue record for this book is available from the British Library.

ISBN: PB: 978-0-7136-6813-1
EPDF: 978-1-4081-4419-0
EPUB: 978-1-4081-4420-6

Library of Congress Cataloging-in-Publication Data
A catalog record for this book is available from the Library of Congress.

CONTENTS

ACKNOWLEDGMENTS

This edition has been built on the foundation of Andor Gomme's previous New Mermaids edition of *The Roaring Girl*. I have retained a great many of his excellent notes and agreed with many of his editorial decisions. I have also had frequent and grateful recourse to the other editions of the play mentioned in the list of Abbreviations. I am particularly indebted to Paul Mulholland's edition for the Revels Plays series and to Cyrus Hoy's annotations to Fredson Bowers's edition.

I am grateful to the Theatre Museum in London for their help in obtaining information about recent productions and for the use of their library. The Shakespeare Library in Stratford-upon-Avon kindly enabled me to watch a video recording of the 1983 production.

I would also like to thank Nick Stafford for lending me the text of his unpublished play, *Moll Cutpurse*, Margaret Berrill, the copy-editor of this volume, for her helpful suggestions, and Brian Gibbons for his friendly and knowledgable advice at every stage.

E.C.

ABBREVIATIONS

Editions of *The Roaring Girl*

Q	The first edition (quarto), London, 1611
Reed	Isaac Reed, ed., R. Dodsley, *A Select Collection of Old Plays*, 2nd edn, 12 vols, London, 1780, vol. VI
Collier	J. P. Collier, ed., R. Dodsley, *A Select Collection of Old Plays*, 3rd edn, 12 vols, London, 1825–7, vol. VI
Dyce	A. Dyce, ed., *The Works of Thomas Middleton*, 5 vols, London, 1840, vol. II
Bullen	A. H. Bullen, ed., *The Works of Thomas Middleton*, 8 vols, London, 1885, vol. IV
Bowers	Fredson Bowers, ed., *The Dramatic Works of Thomas Dekker*, 4 vols, Cambridge, 1953–61, vol. III
Gomme	Andor Gomme, ed., Thomas Middleton and Thomas Dekker, *The Roaring Girl*, London, 1976
Mulholland	Paul Mulholland, ed., Thomas Middleton and Thomas Dekker, *The Roaring Girl*, Manchester, 1987

Other Works

Bald (Chronology)	R. C. Bald, 'The Chronology of Middleton's Plays', *Modern Language Review*, 32 (1937), 33–43
Chambers	E. K. Chambers, *The Elizabethan Stage*, 4 vols, Oxford, 1923, repr: 1974
Hoy	Cyrus Hoy, *Introductions, Notes, and Commentaries to texts in 'The Dramatic Works of Thomas Dekker'*, 4 vols, Cambridge, 1980
OED	*The Oxford English Dictionary*
Sh. Eng.	Walter Ralegh et al., eds, *Shakespeare's England*, 2 vols, Oxford, 1917
Sugden	E. H. Sugden, *A Topographical Dictionary to the Works of Shakespeare and His Fellow Dramatists*, Manchester, 1925

Journals

E in C	*Essays in Criticism*
ELH	*English Literary History*
ELR	*English Literary Renaissance*
MLN	*Modern Language Notes*
MLR	*Modern Language Review*
N&Q	*Notes and Queries*
RES	*Review of English Studies*

SEL   *Studies in English Literature*
SP   *Studies in Philology*

Other Abbreviations

E.C.   Elizabeth Cook (the present editor)
ed.   editor, edited by
qu.   quoted by or in
sd   stage direction
sp   speech prefix

All Shakespeare references are to *The Riverside Shakespeare*, Boston, 1974.

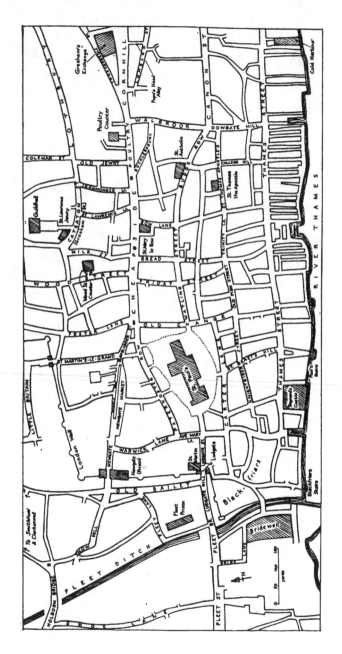

Central London in the early seventeenth century

INTRODUCTION

THE AUTHORS

THOMAS MIDDLETON was a Londoner. He was born in 1580, probably in Limehouse where his father, William Middleton, a builder, owned or leased two properties. He was baptised on 18 April 1580 at St Lawrence Jewry.[1] In January 1585, when Thomas was about five, his father died. Anne Middleton, his mother, found a new husband almost immediately: one Thomas Harvey, 'Citizen and Grocer of London'. Harvey had lost all his money that same year having set out on Ralegh and Grenville's unsuccessful expedition to colonise Roanoke Island. He was a financial adventurer in marriage too: in marrying Anne, he appears to have set his sights on William Middleton's property. Thomas's sister, Avice, also married (in 1586) a man after her late father's property. Legal disputes over property dogged the family for many years. It is not hard to see how this experience fed into Middleton's plays.

In 1598 Thomas Middleton entered Queen's College, Oxford, and during his time there he published three poems including *Micro-Cynicon* (1599), six 'snarling satyres' against vice, and *The Ghost of Lucrece* (1600). In order to subsidise his study he sold part of his share in the family property in 1600 to his brother-in-law, Allen Waterer.

It appears that Middleton did not graduate from Queen's College, having had to return to London to assist his mother in a lawsuit. In February 1600 it is reported that he 'nowe ... remaynethe heare in London daylie accompaninge the players'.[2] At about the same time he married the sister of one of the actors in the Admiral's Men company. Her name was Maulyn ('Maul' or 'Moll', Magdalen or Mary – all variants on the same name) Marbeck. The family had Calvinist as well as musical connections. In 1604 a son, Edward, was born.

In 1602 Henslowe records Middleton's connection with the Admiral's Men and the Earl of Worcester's Men. In this year Middleton collaborated with Anthony Munday, Thomas Drayton,

---

[1] This church was destroyed in the Great Fire of London, 1666, and is not the present St Lawrence Jewry, which was designed by Wren.

[2] Philip Bond, a witness in the family lawsuit, made this statement in a deposition dated 8 February 1600. See P. G. Philias, 'Middleton's Early Contact with the Law', *SP*, 70 (1955), 186–94. The quotation is on p. 192.

John Webster, and Dekker on a now lost play, *Caesar's Fall,* and contributed a prologue and an epilogue for a court performance of Robert Greene's *Friar Bacon and Friar Bungay.* His first known solo composition for the stage, *The Phoenix,* was written, also in 1602, for the Children of Paul's, one of the two principal boys' companies. Here he established his reputation to become, along with Chapman, Marston, and Jonson, one of the foremost writers for boys, producing a number of 'city comedies' including *A Mad World, My Masters.*

While the London theatres were closed on account of the plague, Middleton, like Dekker and several others, turned his hand to pamphlet-writing. In *The Black Book* (1604) he itemises the sins of bawdy-houses and eating-places (ordinaries). As a catalogue of rogue life it was good grounding for *The Roaring Girl.*

By 1604 Middleton had begun to write for the adult companies. The first part of *The Honest Whore* (1604?), co-written with Dekker, was written for Prince Henry's Men (the Admiral's Men re-named) at the Fortune, as was *The Roaring Girl. A Chaste Maid in Cheapside* (1611?) was written for the Lady Elizabeth's Company at the Swan; but most of his work from about 1606 was for the King's Men at the Globe, the company for whom Shakespeare also wrote.

Middleton was very much of the city which he wrote about. He was a practical, working writer. He produced several civic works including, in 1613, the words for an entertainment to mark the installation of his namesake, Sir Thomas Middleton, as Lord Mayor of London and the opening of the New River, the public water system constructed by another Middleton, Hugh. He also wrote the words for several City pageants and masques and was appointed Chronologer of the City of London – a kind of poet laureate of the City – on 6 September 1620.

He seems to have conducted his life with an unsentimental pragmatism and this is reflected in writing which is often shocking in its flat truth-telling. An exchange in *The Changeling* (co-written with Rowley) epitomises his manner. Alsemero accuses De Flores of murdering Piracquo at Beatrice–Joanna's prompting:

> My wife's beforehand with you, she tells me,
> For a brave bloody blow you gave for her sake
> Upon Piracquo.
> DE FLORES   Upon? 'Twas quite through him, sure. (V.iii.103–5)[3]

Women are set at the centre of Middleton's plays. These women,

---

[3] There is a much lighter exchange, which still shows the same cast of mind, in *The Honest Whore,* Part I (another Middleton and Dekker collaboration): Roger, a bawd, accused of being 'slave to sixpence' retorts indignantly, 'Sixpence? Nay, that's not so; I never took under two shillings' (III.ii.50).

whether heroines or villains, are complex, wilful, and self-deter-
mining. Indeed the psychological complexity of a Beatrice–Joanna
belies any easy demarcation between heroine and villain. His char-
acterisations are simultaneously remorseless and compassionate.

During his lifetime his most popular plays included *Hengist, King
of Kent, or The Mayor of Queenborough* (c. 1616) and *A Game at
Chess* (1624): the latter – a political allegory which aimed at James
I's alliance with Spain – was a roaring success and had the longest
known run of any Jacobean play until the Spanish ambassador de-
manded that it be stopped. The company was summoned before
the Privy Council but Middleton failed to appear. His son Edward
was summoned and the players imprisoned but it seems the action
was soon dropped.[4]

A Game at Chess was his last known play. He died in 1627 and
was buried on 4 July at St Mary's, Newington Butts. He seems to
have lived in this area since at least 1609.

Until the early nineteenth century he was considered as just one
of many jobbing dramatists. Now he is regarded as one of the greatest playwrights of his age. His steady gaze, which searches for what
is really so when popular pieties and evasion are stripped away,
feels very contemporary.[5]

Thomas Dekker was also a Londoner but his name and sympa-
thies suggest that his parentage was Dutch. In 1632 he refers to his
'three score years'[6] which would suggest a birth-date around 1572.
It is likely that he began to write for the theatre in the early 1590s
when he was one of many writers collaborating on the unpublished
play, *Sir Thomas More*. Later in this decade he appears as one of the
stable of writers employed by Philip Henslowe to keep the
Admiral's Men and their eager audiences well supplied.[7] Between
1598 and 1602 Dekker was extremely productive, writing for the
Admiral's Men at the Rose and Fortune theatres and later for the
Earl of Worcester's Men at the Rose; he also wrote for the

---

[4] David L. Frost mentions a 'late tradition' that 'Middleton was himself imprisoned
for a while', *The Selected Plays of Thomas Middleton*, ed. David L. Frost, Cambridge,
1978, p. xiv.

[5] In 1986 a reworking by Howard Barker of *Women Beware Women* was put on at the
Royal Court Theatre, London. This was not a half-hearted 'modernisation' of the
play but a collaboration across the centuries.

[6] In the 'Epistle Dedicatory' to *English Villainies*

[7] John C. Meagher writes, 'in a typical fortnight in 1597 the Admiral's Men gave
twelve performances which presented eight to ten different plays ... such a pace de-
manded a constant supply of new plays', 'Hackwriting and the Huntingdon Plays', in
Elizabethan Theatre, Stratford-upon-Avon Studies, 9, London, 1966, 197.

Chamberlain's Men (*Satiromastix*) and for the Children of Paul's (Paul's Boys). He wrote or co-wrote over forty plays.

Like Middleton he turned to pamphlet-writing when plague closed the theatres in 1603. In this he proved a brilliant successor to Thomas Nashe. His *A Knight's Conjuring* (1607) was, like Middleton's *The Black Booke*, written in response to Nashe's *Pierce Pennilesses Supplication to the Devil* (1592).[8] His *The Wonderful Yeare* (1603) commemorates Queen Elizabeth and the many subjects who died of the plague. It ends with fictional sketches. Like Nashe before him and Defoe after, Dekker is one of the creators of a genre we would now call 'faction', combining fiction and reportage to examine recent history. From 1606 he began to write prose pamphlets almost exclusively. These pamphlets show a deep engagement with the life of the city; an awareness of mercantile stratagems and also of the terrible suffering created by poverty: a poverty both exacerbated and thrown into relief by a court which was arrogantly extravagant and anti-populist.

Dekker's compassion for the hungry and powerless went along with a deep personal faith. In 1609 he published *The Four Birds of Noah's Ark*, a collection of prayers. He embraced a form of militant Protestantism which put him increasingly at odds with the policies of Elizabeth and her successor James. Dekker's *The Whore of Babylon* (1605) is described by Julia Gasper as 'the definitive militant Protestant play'.[9] It includes a covert analogy made between Elizabeth – once the great Protestant figurehead – and Nero. In executing Essex, Elizabeth had dealt a terrible blow to the Protestant cause.

Gasper writes: 'Dekker's career as a playwright was a reckless one because he could not depart from his principles. Not only do his plays provide an extensive commentary on the acts of three successive monarchs ... they participate energetically in religious and political affairs, attacking, defending, satirising.'[10]

Dekker himself knew poverty and hardship at first hand. He was thrice imprisoned for debt. Twice – in 1597/8 and on 30 January 1598/9 – Henslowe bailed him out. But in 1613 he was placed in the King's Bench prison, where he stayed for seven years.

He married twice: first, an Elizabeth by whom he had three daughters, Dorcas, Elizabeth, and Anne, who were baptised at

---

[8] *Thomas Dekker's 'A Knights Conjuring' (1607): A Critical Edition*, ed. Larry M. Robbins, The Hague, 1974. The Introduction to this edition provides much useful information about Dekker.

[9] Julia Gasper, *The Dragon and the Dove: The Plays of Thomas Dekker*, Oxford, 1990, p. 62

[10] Ibid., p. 10

St Giles, Cripplegate, in 1594, 1598, and 1602. His second wife, whose name, like Middleton's wife's, was Mary, was buried on 24 July 1616.

His play *Match me in London*, written around 1621, has a heroine whose radical chastity has something in common with Moll. She would rather kill a monarch than be a whore and she is armed with a stiletto and poniard.

Like Middleton, Dekker had some involvement with civic pageants. He also wrote a masque, with John Ford, for the Lady Elizabeth's Company which was significantly, and unusually for a masque, put on at a public theatre, the Cockpit, and not at court.

In 1626, along with Webster, Rowley, and Ford, Dekker appeared in the Star Chamber in a libel case associated with the play *Keep the Widow Waking*. The case continued for two years. Dekker seems to have given up writing for the stage at this point. He died, probably in debt, in 1632.

While his pamphlets have long been read and appreciated for the intricate information they provide about London life, that appreciation has been mixed with a degree of condescension. Dekker has been seen as the sweet cheery chappie of Elizabethan and Jacobean literature – a view based principally on a reading of his best-known play, *The Shoemaker's Holiday*. Swinburne admired his poetry but questioned his 'constructive power'.[11] To T. S. Eliot, whose admiration of *The Roaring Girl* did much to revive its fortunes, 'Dekker is all sentiment'.[12] Dekker's populism, which informs *The Roaring Girl*, needs to be seen as an expression of his belief in the inviolable worth of each person, regardless of status, and in the context of a conspicuously un-populist monarchy.

DATE, SOURCES, AND AFTERLIFE

The dating of the play is assisted by a record of Mary Frith's conduct in *The Consistory of London Correction Book* dated 27 January 1611:

> This day and place the said Mary appeared personally and then and there voluntarily confessed that she had long frequented all or most of the disorderly and licentious places in this City as namely she hath usually in the habit of a man resorted to alehouses Taverns Tobacco shops and also to play houses there to see plays and prizes and namely being at a play about 3 quarters of a year since at the Fortune in mans apparel and in her boots and with a sword by her side, she told the company there present that she thought many of

---

[11] See Sara Jayne Steen, *Ambrosia in an Earthen Vessel: Three Centuries of Audience and Reader Response to the Works of Thomas Middleton*, New York, 1993, p. 167.

[12] T. S. Eliot, in 'Thomas Middleton', in *Elizabethan Essays*, London, 1927, p. 96

them were of opinion that she was a man, but if any of them would come to her lodging they should find that she is a woman and some other immodest and lascivious speeches she also used at that time And also sat there upon the stage in the public view of all the people there present in mans apparel and played upon her lute and sang a song. And she further confessed that she hath for this long time past usually blasphemed and dishonored the name of God by swearing and cursing and by tearing God out of his kingdom if it were possible, and hath also usually associated her self with Ruffianly swaggering and lewd company as namely with cut purses blasphemous drunkards and others of bad note and of most dissolute behaviour with whom she hath to the great shame of her sex often times (as she said) drunk hard and distempered her head with drink And further confesseth that since she was punished for the misdemeanours afore mentioned in Bridewell she was since upon Christmas day at night taken in Pauls Church with her petticoat tucked up about her in the fashion of a man with a mans cloak on her to the great scandal of divers persons who understood the same and to the disgrace of all womanhood And she sayeth and protesteth that she is heartily sorry for her foresaid licentious and dissolute life and giveth her earnest promise to carry and behave her self ever from hence forward honestly soberly and womanly and resteth ready to undergo any censure or punishment for her misdemeanours aforesaid in such manner and form as shall be assigned her ... And then she being pressed to declare whether she had not been dishonest of her body and hath not also drawn other women to lewdness by her persuasions and by carrying her self like a bawd, she absolutely denied that she was chargeable with either of these imputations.[13]

It seems more than probable that the play which Moll attended at the Fortune Theatre, and at which she played her lute and sang, was *The Roaring Girl*. She would thereby have fulfilled the promise of the Epilogue that 'The Roaring Girl herself some few days hence, / Shall on this stage give larger recompense.' Perhaps, as Mulholland suggests, Mary Frith actually stood in at some point for the actor representing her.[14] IV.i, where Moll accompanies herself on a viol, is the most likely point in the play for this to have occurred.

Gull's words to Jack Dapper about a 'great fellow' with 'fair sword and buckler' who was 'dry-beat ... with a cudgel' by a butcher (III.iii.204–6) may well refer to an incident in February 1611, when two butchers were accused of assaulting gentlemen at the Fortune.[15] It would seem that *The Roaring Girl* was written after this last incident and not long before the *Correction Book* entry

---

[13] I have modernised the spelling of this text which is printed in full in P. A. Mulholland, 'The Date of *The Roaring Girl*', *RES,* new series 28, (1977), 30–1. The previous misdating of this document had led to an earlier date being attributed to *The Roaring Girl.*

[14] Ibid., p. 22

[15] Chambers, II, 441

which refers to Moll's appearance at the Fortune as if it were recent history.

R. C. Bald has identified the book '(Foul as his brains they flowed from)' mentioned in the Epilogue, l.23, as Samuel Rid's ('S. R.') *Martin Mark-All, Beadle of Bridewell; His Defence and Answer to the Bellman of London*, a pamphlet registered on 31 March 1610, which disparaged Dekker's recent work and questioned his knowledge of thieves' cant.[16] This identification confirms that *The Roaring Girl* was written after S. R.'s pamphlet.

Two other factors, noted first by Mulholland, point to 1611 as the play's date. Moll's analogy between her own knowledge of the underworld and the knowledge of a gentleman recently returned from Venice with inside information about the tricks of courtesans (V.i.318ff.) is likely to have been suggested by Thomas Coryat's description of Venetian courtesans in his recently published *Crudities*,[17] entered in the Stationers' Register on 26 November 1610, dated 1611 on the title-page). Prince Henry, who had financed the publication of the *Crudities*, was also patron of the Prince's Men who played at the Fortune. Lastly, the reference to a new play at the Swan Theatre (in V.i.289) precludes a date earlier than 1611, since for about a decade prior to 1611 the theatre had been used for other kinds of entertainments.

The principal armature of the play's plot – parent-thwarted young lovers succeeding through resourcefulness – is standard for romantic comedy. For some specific details of incident and language there are precedents and sources.[18] A now lost play, *Long Meg*, dramatised the exploits of Long Meg of Westminster, an armed and sometimes cross-dressed female champion of the poor.[19] The image of the goddess Diana stands behind any portrayal of an active and valiant female chastity and the cult of Astraea surrounding Elizabeth, the virgin queen, had made such images more familiar.[20] While Middleton and Dekker had both explored the underworld in their pamphlet writings, Dekker's *Bellman of London* and its sequel, *Lanthorn and Candlelight*, inform the canting scene in V.i.

But it is the living figure of Mary Frith (1584?–1659) who is the

[16] Bald (Chronology), pp. 37–9
[17] See P. A. Mulholland, 'The Date of *The Roaring Girl*', p. 28.
[18] See Bald (Chronology).
[19] Though the play is lost, an anonymous prose work, *The Life of Long Meg of Westminster*, 1620, survives. Mulholland prints an excerpt from it in an Appendix to his Revels edition of *The Roaring Girl*.
[20] Frances A. Yates, *Astraea: The Imperial Theme in the Sixteenth Century*, London, 1975

inspirational heart of the play. Her reputation seems to have been established before Middleton and Dekker's play. In August 1610 a book by John Day is entered into the Stationers' Register: *A Booke called the Madde Pranks of Merry Moll of the Bankside, with her walks in Man's Apparel and to what Purpose.* No copy of this book survives and it is not known to have been printed, but the entry establishes Moll as already A Subject: an item of popular mythology in her own lifetime.

Myth is a collective creation, owned by no-one. Middleton and Dekker's play both draws upon and gives to the mythology surrounding its heroine. To some extent it must have consolidated her notoriety and perhaps enabled a finger-pointing public to think about her with affection, but the myth of Moll Cutpurse is not contained in the play.

The *Correction Book* entry quoted above charges her with offences against convention: drunkenness, swearing, and cross-dressing. Her show of repentance during her public penance may have been a knowing contribution to the street theatre which the occasion provided. She seems to have been a show-woman. John Chamberlain paints the scene in a letter to Dudley Carlton dated 12 February 1612:

> this last Sunday Mall Cut-purse a notorious baggage (that used to go in mans apparel and challenged the field of divers gallants) was brought to [Paul's Cross] ... where she wept bitterly and seemed very penitent, but it is since doubted that she was maudlin drunk, being discovered to have tippled three quarts of sack before she came to her penance: she had the daintiest preacher ... I ever saw in pulpit ... he did extreme badly, and so wearied the audience that the best part went away, and the rest tarried rather to hear Mall Cut-purse than him.[21]

She is referred to in Dekker's *If this be not a good play, the Devil is in it* (also 1611): Pluto asks an assembly of devils if Mall Cutpurse – his 'daughter' and their 'cousin' – has yet arrived in hell. Shacklesoule replies, ' 'Tis not yet fit *Mall Cutpurse* here should hole, / She has been too late a sore-tormented soul' (V.iv.107–8). Another devil, Lurch, says 'Mall Cutpurse plies her task and cannot come' (l.112). It would seem she was still doing her penance at the time of this play.

In 1614 the following epigram by Thomas Freeman appeared in *Rubbe and a Great Cast*:

> They say Moll's honest, and it may be so,
> But yet it is a shrewd presumption, no;
> To touch but pitch, 'tis known it will defile,

---

[21] Quoted by Cyrus Hoy in his Introduction to *The Roaring Girl*. I have modernised the spelling.

Moll wears the breech, what may she be the while;
Sure she that doth the shadow so much grace,
What will she when the substance comes in place.[22]

In 1618 she appears in *Amends for Ladies*, a comedy by Nathaniel
Field, sent by Sir John Lovall to procure the virtuous Grace
Seldom. Grace, who addresses Moll as 'Mistress *hic* and *haec*',
sends her packing:

Hence lewd impudent
I know not what to tearme thee, man or woman,
For nature shaming to acknowledge thee
For either; hath produc'd thee to the World
Without a sex, some say thou art a woman,
Others a man, and many thou art both
Woman and man, but I thinke rather neither
Or man and horse, as the old Centaures were faign'd.[23]

In a play by Brown, *The Court Beggar* (1632), the 'honest Moll' of
The Roaring Girl is referred to; when the character Citwit is robbed
of his watch he says he will seek out Moll to retrieve it.

In 1662 a work claiming to be partly autobiographical, *The Life
and Death of Mrs. Mary Frith, commonly called Moll Cutpurse*, was
published, as well as a shorter work, tellingly titled *The Woman's
Champion*, based on the same source material. Here we learn that
as a child she resisted all discipline and had proved a 'very tomrig
and rumpscuttle'; she 'delighted and sorted only in boys' plays and
pastime'.[24] When she had grown into a 'lusty and sturdy wench'
she was sent out into domestic service but she disliked housework
and had a 'natural abhorrence to the tending of children'. Having
abandoned domestic service she dressed in masculine fashion and
became notorious as cutpurse, receiver, forger, and fortune-teller;
she numbered highwaymen among her friends.

In common with Middleton and Dekker's Moll, the Moll of the
Life presents herself as without sexual desire. Here, however, her
celibacy is given no active moral dimension. 'The apathy and in-
sensibleness of my carnal pleasures even to stupidity possessed
me'.[25] She does not identify with the male transvestite, Aniseed-
water Robin, in some spirit of solidarity with the marginal. Far

---

[22] Thomas Freeman, *Rubbe and a Great Cast, The Second Bowle*, 1614
[23] *Amends for Ladies with the Humour of Roring*, 1618, sig. C2
[24] *The Life and Death of Mrs. Mary Frith, commonly called Moll Cutpurse*, 1662, ed.
Randall S. Nakayama, New York, 1993, pp. 10, 13
[25] Ibid., p. 58

from it. He fills her with 'so strange an antipathy' that she gets her boys to fall upon him and throw dirt at him.[26]

Like Middleton and Dekker's Moll, the Moll of the *Life* has her own sense of justice. She receives stolen goods and then sells them back to their legal owners; she gets fathers to pay up for their illegitimate children.[27]

She was a royalist and, with political consistency, once robbed General Fairfax and shot him in the arm on Hounslow Heath. For this she was sent to Newgate but she procured her release by paying Fairfax the huge sum of £2,000. She worked with a well-trained dog and smoked a lot. It was this habit of smoking which was thought to have kept her alive for so long. In later life she blew up with 'the dropsy'.

The myth of Moll Cutpurse continues. Defoe's Moll Flanders describes herself as 'as impudent a thief and as dextrous as ever Moll Cut-Purse was'.[28] More recent treatments have denied her her celibacy: she has become the actively lesbian heroine of Ellen Galford's novel *Moll Cutpurse*,[29] and the bisexual heroine of a play by Nick Stafford, who interprets Moll's pleasure in 'both sides o'th'bed' (II.ii.37) as an indication that she is AC/DC.[30] Both of these works feature Thomas Middleton but leave out Dekker.

Perhaps the most interesting recent appearance of Moll is in the fantasy novels of Michael Scott Rohan, *Chase the Morning* (1990) and *Cloud Castles* (1993), where she is introduced as Mad Mall, an asexual, magical figure liberated from history in the tradition that includes Ariel and Mr Spock.

THE PLAY IN PERFORMANCE

In the second scene of the play Sir Alexander Wengrave, in the course of showing off his expensive new home and furnishings to his friends, invites his guests to 'look into my galleries'. It is an obvious cue for the actor playing Sir Alexander to gesture

[26] Ibid., p. 46
[27] According to M. Dowlings, the historical Mary Frith held a royal commission to examine people arrested for petty crimes, so she did later use her knowledge of lawlessness in the service of law. 'A Note on Moll Cutpurse', *RES*, 10 (1934), 67–71
[28] Daniel Defoe, *Moll Flanders* (1722), London, 1972, p. 173
[29] Ellen Galford, *Moll Cutpurse: Her True History*, 1984 (by Stramullion Cooperative) and London, 1993
[30] Nick Stafford's *Moll Cutpurse* was first played in 1989 by the Avon Touring Company at the Bristol Montpelier Centre, and then at the Drill Hall, London, by Perspectives Company in 1991.

towards the audience beyond: the edifice of the theatre becomes
his house; the audience, the crowded and lifelike pictures he has
collected:[31]

> Within one square a thousand heads are laid
> So close that all of heads the room seems made   (19–20)

Turning the tables on the audience, he makes them the objects of
scrutiny, yet his description also indicates – perhaps proleptically –
their responsiveness:

> As many faces there, filled with blithe looks,
> Show like the promising titles of new books
> Writ merrily, the readers being their own eyes,
> Which seem to move and to give plaudities   (21–4)

In the 1983 Royal Shakespeare Company production of this play
the actor scanned the audience as he spoke these lines, making the
auditorium of the Shakespeare Memorial Theatre the galleries of
Sir Alexander's overcrowded house. In the Fortune, the theatre in
which *The Roaring Girl* was first performed, the projecting stage
would have given the actor virtually nowhere else to turn but to the
surrounding audience.

This projecting stage was 43 feet wide and 27½ feet deep (ap-
proximately 13 metres by 9 metres) and was surrounded on three
sides by galleries. Parts of the galleries were partitioned off and
given ceilings to become 'gentlemen's rooms'. Unlike the Globe
and the Swan, the building was rectangular. It was commissioned
by Henslowe and Alleyn to emulate and rival the Globe, 'the last
new thing in theatres', and built by the same man, Peter Street.[32]
The specifications for building include many references to the
Globe; among the distinguishing new features of the Fortune are
carvings of satyrs on the main posts of stage and auditorium. It was
clearly quite a fancy theatre and one of which a Sir Alexander
would be proud.

The location of the Fortune on the north-west boundary of the
City, between Golden Lane and Whitecross Street, was convenient
for the prosperous inhabitants of the suburbs. Indeed, it was well
placed to attract as great a cross-section of the population as the
play depicts. Sometimes the results were inflammatory: as in the
February 1611 incident of the two butchers charged with abusing
gentlemen at the theatre.[33]

[31] M. W. Sampson, *MLN*, 30 (1915), 195
[32] Chambers, II, 435–40. See also Richard Hosley, 'A Reconstruction of the Fortune
Playhouse', in G. R. Hibbard, ed., *The Elizabethan Theatre*, VI, 1978, pp. 1–20 and
The Elizabethan Theatre, VII, 1980, pp. 1–20.
[33] See above, p. xviii.

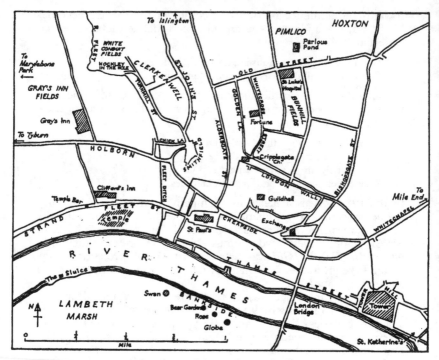

London and the northern suburbs

Like other theatres, the Fortune also offered rich pickings for cutpurses. In V.i.269–70 Moll identifies one of the cutpurses she encounters as one she once 'took . . . i'the twopenny gallery at the Fortune': the fact that the historical Moll Frith is known to have frequented this theatre confirms the underworld link. Her fictional representation on stage exists to chastise the likes of her historical self.

A trapdoor was a standard part of Elizabethan stage design, and the presence of a character named Trapdoor seems to require the use of such a stage property. Trapdoor's appearance from and disappearance into his namesake – an opening in the stage into the below-stage area known as 'hell' – would have accentuated the infernal atmosphere he carries with him.[34] In the Fortune Theatre

[34] Chambers, II, 528

this area was closed from the audience's view. I think it is probable that his first two entrances were made on to the stage through the trapdoor. On both occasions he is asked not *who* he is, but *what* he is ('Now sirrah, what are you?' (I.ii.186); 'How now, what art thou?' (II.i.326)). The pronoun suggests that the manner of his appearing throws his humanity into question.

Thomas Middleton, in introducing his 'published comedy', recommends it as a book to be read as much as a play to be performed: '[it] may be allowed both gallery room at the playhouse, and chamber room at your lodging'. According a play-script the respectable status of a book – something to be kept and read over – was relatively new in 1611. The meticulous editorial care which Ben Jonson bestowed upon his plays made a novel claim for the dignity of contemporary drama. But Middleton was prescient in recommending his play to readers since, until recently, *The Roaring Girl* has been more read, and edited, than performed. Sir Walter Scott knew it and so, later in the nineteenth century, did Trollope, who, having scanned it for elements which he could lift for his own purposes, deemed it 'a most unintelligible gallimafrey, unreadable as a whole ... but with sparkles of such wit as was then popular'.[35] Trollope seems to have read, and judged, the play as if it were a novel. Swinburne, a little later, esteemed it as poetry.[36] But while philologists and writers certainly read the play and perhaps performed it in the theatres of their minds, there is no record of any theatrical production of *The Roaring Girl* between 1611 and April 1951, when it was performed by the Brattle Theatre Company, Massachusetts, as a Restoration period piece. In 1956 the BBC Third Programme produced it as a radio play.

The growth of the women's movement is largely behind the relative frequency with which it has been revived in recent years. In June 1970 it was performed at the Dundee Repertory, directed by Keith Darvill, with Laura Graham as Moll. It has also been produced by various student companies. In 1979 it was put on at the University of Los Angeles with the subtitle 'a feminist infiltration'; in 1980 the Cambridge Mummers performed it at the Edinburgh Festival, editing the play to focus more clearly on Moll; in 1981 Royal Holloway College, London, produced the play.

But the first major professional stage production of the play since 1611 was that of the Royal Shakespeare Company in 1983, first in Stratford-upon-Avon and then, in April, at the Barbican Centre, London. This production, directed by Barry Kyle and shown in repertory with *The Taming of the Shrew*, which Kyle also directed, starred Helen Mirren as Moll, who played, in the view of one critic,

---

[35] Quoted in Sara Jayne Steen, *Ambrosia in an Earthen Vessel*, p. 123
[36] Ibid., p. 167

'with the swaggering heartiness of a pantomime Robin Hood'.[37] Kyle was interested in the correspondences between Jacobean London and the London of the 1980s. He approached it as if it were a new play; he regarded it as 'a moral comedy about the class system breaking down in a Jacobean world of profiteering and self-interest'.[38] For all the contemporaneity of emphasis, the play was played in period costume while C. Dyer's set was emblematic and included – *Metropolis*-like – a set of cog-wheels to represent Tudor and Stuart capitalism. The busts of Elizabeth and James dominated. While Helen Mirren's presence in the production made it in one sense a star vehicle, Kyle also sought to represent the underclass for whom Moll is spokeswoman. The set was populated not just by actors with speaking parts but by those representing the voiceless cripples, beggars, and hangers-on who live on the leavings; an underworld 'as seen through Puritan eyes'.[39] This production did not lose the eschatological dimension of the play. Jonathan Hyde's Laxton came across as a chillingly diabolical figure. The striking of the clock in III.i.27 carried a sense of reckoning reminiscent of the last scene of Marlowe's *Doctor Faustus*. The reviewers tended to praise the performances rather than the play. The reviewer in the *Sunday Telegraph*, who praised Jonathan Hyde's 'richly odious' performance, noted that productions of *The Roaring Girl* 'are as rare as cuckoos in January ... it is easy to see why'.[40]

They are getting less rare. It was put on again in June 1989 (6th–17th) at the Bristol Theatre Royal, directed by Sonia Fraser. Francesca Hunt played Moll. The play has waited a long time to be heard.

THE COLLECTING CLASSES

In IV.ii Mistress Gallipot and Mistress Openwork, the wives of an apothecary and a sempster respectively, discuss the severe shortcomings of the higher-ranking 'gallants':

MISTRESS OPENWORK
   ... 'las, what are your whisking gallants to our husbands, weigh 'em rightly man for man?
MISTRESS GALLIPOT
   Troth, mere shallow things.

---

[37] Milton Shulman in the *Evening Standard*, 27 April 1983
[38] Interview with Barry Kyle in the *Sunday Times*, 24 April 1983
[39] John Barber in the *Daily Telegraph*, 28 April 1983
[40] *The Sunday Telegraph*, 1 May 1983

MISTRESS OPENWORK

Idle simple things, running heads, and yet let 'em run over us never so fast, we shopkeepers, when all's done, are sure to have 'em in our purse-nets at length, and when they are in, Lord, what simple animals they are. (IV.ii.42–9)

This play, dominated by a singular (and single) woman, is very much concerned with the weighing of men. It is the women who do this; either with the trader's eye for substance, or, in the case of Moll, with a disinterested discernment derived from self-sufficiency, valour, and skill.

We do not meet the shopkeepers until the second act for we are introduced to the ranks of characters in an apparently systematic way of gradual descent; but the shopkeepers' world of buying and selling is, as in many 'city comedies', at the heart of this play and a central description of what human relations have become. Appropriation is what most of the characters in this play are about. We are plunged, in Act I, into a world of conspicuous consumption. Sir Alexander, father to the play's romantic hero Sebastian, is, for all his thrusting and ostentatious hospitality, primarily an acquisitor – of wealth, furniture, pictures, attitudes. Even travel, once the provenance of soldiers, pilgrims, and politicians, has become a consumer commodity, and linguistic accomplishment an object of competitive quantification. Under cover of describing one Master Greenwit, Sir Alexander boasts about his son:

... such a traveller,
He has more tongues in his head than some have teeth. (I.ii.120–1)

The consumers who were this play's first audience did not need to go abroad, or even beyond the City, to encounter new language. In V.i Jack Dapper and Lord Noland listen to Moll, Trapdoor, and Tearcat converse in thieves' cant: 'Zounds', says Jack Dapper, 'I'll give a schoolmaster half a crown a week, and teach me this pedlar's French' (V.i.168–9). Moll obligingly gives her noble companions a crash course in this cant. Her proficiency, she explains, is not evidence of her corruption: she has acquired this knowledge for the sake of alerting the unwary. She compares her situation with that of a visitor to Venice, initiated into 'the close tricks of courtesans' by some pander. On return they would, like herself, 'proclaim / [their] knowledge in those villainies' to a dear friend about to make the same journey, 'to save / Your friend from their quick danger' (V.i.320–5).[41]

In reality thieves' cant – any underworld slang – mutates as fast

---

[41] See p. xix above.

as it can be learnt by outsiders. It lives in exclusion. The newly-learned are left holding the tails of quick lizards who have moved on. This did not deter the Jacobean reading public (greatly expanded by the new middle classes) from consuming with pleasure the 'cony-catching' pamphlets which seemed to give them access to the lingo of the underworld: a little whiff of brimstone from the safety of their majority; the *frisson* of danger along with the comfortable sense that it has been tamed by appropriation.[42]

Other languages are appropriated too – languages of high tragedy, of romantic love, of spiritual reflection. This play is exceptionally full of passages of speech in which the situation fails to motivate the intensity of idiom. The words seem to be lifted from some other context and here have the hollow ring of parody. Sir Alexander, for instance, expressing his disappointment with Sebastian:

> This son ... that should be
> The column and main arch unto my house,
> The crutch unto my age, becomes a whirlwind
> Shaking the firm foundation –   (I.ii.113–16)

Likewise Mistress Gallipot's expression of her erotic dilemma – 'I'm like a needle 'twixt two adamants' (III.ii.72) – sounds booklearnt and parodic. There seems no reason to take these expressions of passion seriously. Like the spoiled coins which Sir Alexander tries to foist on Moll, they aren't quite the real thing.

There is a more uncomfortable excess in the language which Sir Alexander uses to declare his enmity towards his son. The arbitrary craziness anticipates the mad Ferdinand in Webster's *The Duchess of Malfi*:

> ... take thy flight,
> I'll be most near thee when I'm least in sight.
> Wild buck, I'll hunt thee breathless, thou shalt run on,
> But I will turn thee when I'm not thought upon.   (I.ii.182–5)

The axis on which Sir Alexander operates is one of envy. He values what he has on account of the envy he feels it must necessarily engender. It is therefore humiliating to him that Moll, on seeing the watch that he has laid out for her to steal (and thereby incriminate herself), simply observes the time and leaves it (IV.i.128–30). In Sir Alexander and his friend Sir Davy we see the cruel envy of fathers for sons. Each is bent upon thwarting his (slightly) more vital offspring with a malice which is hideous. Sir

---

[42] See Brian Gibbons, *Jacobean City Comedy*, 2nd edn, London, 1980, Appendix, 'A Minor Genre: the Coney-catching Pamphlet'.

Davy attempts to get his son arrested and cast into a debtors' prison. 'I'll make him sing a counter-tenor sure' (III.iii.77). Would he like to see his son castrated too? There is certainly that suggestion. 'A nasty plot' (V.i.43) to be sure.

These two knights, the play's older generation, need to feel that the wealth with which their rank has probably been acquired is to be valued. Their anxiety about how their sons may disperse it betrays a reluctance to relinquish control, even in death. The language of self-shriving is appropriated by Sir Alexander in II.ii. But again, it sounds completely hollow:

> ... I have weightier business of mine own
> Than to chide thee: I must not to my grave
> As a drunkard to his bed, whereon he lies
> Only to sleep, and never cares to rise.   (II.ii.125–8)

The next generation – the 'gallants' – Sebastian, Jack Dapper, Goshawk, Greenwit, and Laxton, are a fairly vacant lot. Sebastian stands out as the most enterprising, least acquisitive, since what he seeks is the choice of his heart. His speeches on the subject are stock and flat but he has the wit to think up a plot which will induce his father to welcome his choice of wife. Yet there is something heartless and unimaginative in his complacent assumption that his pretended choice, Moll Frith, the Roaring Girl, is, by common consent, beyond the pale. He gets a sexual thrill from kissing his strategically cross-dressed sweetheart (IV.i.46–7) whilst making the vocationally cross-dressed Moll into an icon of unacceptability. Like his friends who will savour their taste of underworld cant, he likes his danger safe.

Jack Dapper, imagined by his father to be squandering himself on boys and tobacco (III.iii.58–66), is merely foolish. A collector, like his elders, but of more conspicuously trifling items – a spangled feather (emblem of vanity), a novel word ('Is not amorous a good word?' (V.i.60)). His objects lack solidity; his energy is dissipative and he by nature opposes the consolidating acquisitiveness of his father. This makes him a natural ally to Moll Cutpurse (who is also sometimes called 'Jack').[43] Moll's saving him from the counter (where Dekker had languished) is presented as an unambiguous good.

Laxton and Goshawk's acquisitiveness is more unpleasant, fuelled by the arrogance of gender and rank. Goshawk, in his duplicity towards the Openworks, would sacrifice the candour of

---

[43] Viviana Comensoli writes: 'That Jack functions dramatically as Moll's double is suggested by Moll's street name, "Iack" (V.ii.97; ll.212, 215)', in 'Play-making, Domestic Conduct, and the Multiple Plot' in *The Roaring Girl, SEL*, 27 (1987), 261.

friendship for a covert liaison. Laxton exploits Mistress Gallipot's susceptibility towards him in the hope of financial gain – a reminder that the citizen–shopkeepers might well have access to more wealth than their 'betters'. Though the wit of the shopkeepers limits the harm wrought by Laxton and Goshawk, the motivation of these two is diabolical.[44]

As we descend, by a kind of decorum, through the ranks of characters, the degree of individuation increases.[45] The shopkeepers, whom we first meet in Act II, handle real goods in their daily lives, and their language, correspondingly, has a greater particularity. While Mistress Gallipot's expressions of love for Laxton sound stock and book-learnt, her irritable flashes at her husband are entirely idiosyncratic and real: 'I cannot abide a man that's too fond over me, so cookish' (III.ii.23–4).

Master Gallipot's willingness to pay out to save their marriage is touching. It also indicates that there is a lot of money available. It is to the citizens that the likes of Laxton turn for cash. When his wife feigns distress over Laxton's letter, the order in which his alarmed imagination enlarges is revealing. Has a child died? Are his barns and houses burnt? Has his factor collapsed or has the ship in whose merchandise he has invested sunk? The loss of a ship is more terrible to him than the death of a child. Of course, infant mortality was then much higher: what strikes us as heartless may not have struck the play's first audiences so. Gallipot, with his 'cookish' devotion to his wife, may be more tender-hearted than Sir Davy who would, in Curtilax's estimation, flay off the skin of his dead father 'if he were sure [it] would yield him any money ... and sell it to cover drums for children at Bartholomew Fair' (III.iii.155–8). Nevertheless, they both have an eye to the main chance.

The vertical descent through the ranks of these three groups of characters is interrupted by the arrival of Trapdoor, perhaps from below,[46] at the end of Act I. He, with his branded hand, has infernal associations. His name links him to the 'hell' of earlier drama – the trapdoor through which Marlowe's Mephistophilis would have appeared and through which Faustus eventually falls to damnation. His ancestry stretches back ultimately to the mystery cycles. In this secular city, however, the infernal has been naturalised as the underworld. Just as the shops and shopkeepers are emblematic of the acquisitive and retentive habits of other characters in the play, so

---

[44] Goshawk's abuse of friendship links him with Iago.
[45] A comparable descent through rank and ascent in linguistic particularity occurs in Shakespeare's *A Midsummer Night's Dream*.
[46] See above, p. xxiv.

Trapdoor's fairly blatant hellishness emblematises and points our attention towards the diabolical intentions that operate elsewhere in the play. In both cases the emblems are less guilty of what they represent – since they do it 'honestly' – than the characters whose acquisitiveness and destructiveness are less overt.

Trapdoor, Tearcat, Moll Cutpurse, form a group only by default: they are more marginal and less circumscribed than the gentry and the citizens. While the other characters traipse docilely out to areas of recreation – to Hoxton, Pimlico, or Brentford – these lead less demarcated lives.

M. F.: THE UNCLASSIFIED

Most of the characters in this play, like those in the medieval Morality tradition in which 'city comedy' is rooted, can be classed as types, but Trapdoor's anarchic arrival signals the breakdown of classification. The only truly singular character, however, is Moll. She, by her singularity, becomes the measure against which others can be valued. She calls the bluff of those who seem bent on the acquisition of novelty – chairs with backs to them, *trompe l'oeil* paintings, spangled feathers, interesting words. She alone is authentic in her difference. Sir Alexander, for all his modish pursuit of the new, has no wish to really stand out and be different: if he did, Moll would be the daughter-in-law of his dreams:

> You had no note before, an unmarked knight;
> Now all the town will take regard on you   (V.ii.154–5)

Moll is 'a thing / One knows not how to name' (I.ii.128–9). To name is to classify and Moll eludes classification.

But 'Moll', the name which fails to name her, is, as the play recognises, a by-word for 'woman'.[47] It is a name shared by the woman who is in some ways her antithesis, Sebastian's sweetheart, Mary Fitz-Allard (see p. xiii). May it have been conscious on the parts of Middleton and Dekker that the play's two juxtaposed heroines, Moll Frith and Mary Fitz-Allard, share not only first names but also the initials M. F.? Moll Frith's name was a historical given, but Mary Fitz-Allard's name was a matter of choice. Both women (played originally of course by boys) cross-dress. Both M. F.s are Male as well as Female.

This play engages with a concern, voiced with increasing frequency in James's England, about the nature of masculine and feminine. Queen Elizabeth I, Amazonian in her strength and com-

---

[47] Both Middleton and Dekker were married to women named Mary.

bativeness ('I have the heart and stomach of a king') had been succeeded in 1603 by James I with his pacifist ideology and homoerotic milieu. Women had long cross-dressed for motives of expediency – for comfort whilst travelling and the safety of disguise –[48] but the positive fashion of cross-dressing by women is first commented upon in the 1570s. Comments on the subject are, Linda Woodbridge notes, nearly always accompanied by remarks on male effeminacy.[49] It is as if a certain quota of masculinity were available: if men did not avail themselves fully of it, women had to take up the slack. While there is little comment on transvestism during the 1590s and early 1600s, by 1615 it is clearly a substantial practice. Thomas Adams, in his *Mystical Bedlam*, writes, '*Hic mulier* will shortly be good Latine, if this transmigration hold.'[50]

1604 marked the repeal of sumptuary law: law which prescribed entitlement to wear certain fabrics, colours, and garments. With the merchant purveyors of rich fabrics often more able to afford those fabrics than their social superiors, the elaborate, cost-entwined symbolism of sumptuary law had gone haywire.[51] James's notorious sale of knighthoods and, after 1615, of peerages, involved the creation of a new aristocracy. During the first two decades of the seventeenth century it was probably harder to 'place' a person than ever before – a source of great anxiety for those of conservative temperament. With so many of the old signifiers empty, where could one find a true sign? Many shared Philip Stubbes's view that 'our Apparell was giuen vs as a signe distinctiue to discerne betwixt sex and sex'.[52] Recorded reactions to cross-dressed women betray a fear that licence in dress is part of a more general licentiousness.[53] Loose, long hair had traditionally been construed as sexually provocative. Now, when women began to crop their hair, it was redescribed: a modest woman would use long hair to screen her breasts from view. James, though himself an influential participant

[48] See Rudolf M. Dekker and Lotte C. Van de Pol, *The Tradition of Female Transvestism in Early Modern Europe*, Basingstoke, 1989, pp. 6–8.
[49] Linda Woodbridge, *Women and the English Renaissance: Literature and the Nature of Womankind 1540–1620*, Brighton, 1984, p. 141
[50] Thomas Adams, *Mystical Bedlam, or the World of Mad-men*, 1615, quoted in Woodbridge, *Women and the English Renaissance*, p. 142. The Latin *hic* and *haec* are, respectively, the Nominative masculine and feminine words for 'this'. Thus '*hic mulier*' means something like 'this he-woman'; '*haec vir*', 'this she-man'.
[51] See Lisa Jardine, *Still Harping on Daughters: Women and Drama in the Age of Shakespeare*, 2nd edn, New York, 1983, chapter 5. On pp. 142–4 sumptuary law is summarised in table form.
[52] Philip Stubbes, *Anatomy of Abuses*, 1583, sig. F5, quoted in Woodbridge, *Women and the English Renaissance*, p. 140
[53] Woodbridge, *Women and the English Renaissance*, p. 144

in a trend which feminised the masculine, asked the Bishop of London in 1620, 'to inveigh vehemently ... against the insolencie of our women and theyre wearing of brode brimd hats, pointed dublets, theyre haire cut short or shorne, and some of them stilettaes or poinards'.[54] In the same year, 1620, two anonymous pamphlets appeared. The first, *Hic Mulier: or, the Man Woman*, links cross-dressing with sexual licence and sees it as a threat to social stability. The second, *Haec Vir: or, the Womanly Man*, a reply issued seven days later, takes the form of a dialogue between the masculine woman and the feminine man. In it the Hic Mulier figure gives voice to a woman's equal claim to humanity and instinctual fulfilment. At the end, however, Hic Mulier seems to swallow her own arguments by implicating the feminisation of men in her, and her fellows', adoption of masculine ways: 'Hence we have preserved ... those manly things which you have forsaken, which would you againe accept ... doubt not but chaste thoughts and bashfulnesse will againe dwell in us.'[55]

The critique of contemporary masculinity, which becomes explicit in the *Haec Vir* pamphlet nine years later, runs through *The Roaring Girl*. The majority of the play's male characters are 'all mouth and trousers'. They are quick to brag, slow to fight. There is a soldier but no war (Trapdoor) and a 'gallant' (Laxton) who employs the language of seduction whilst in flight from opportunity. Counterfeit soldiers, counterfeit lovers, counterfeit words, and, from Sir Alexander, counterfeit coin. While Moll's celibacy is vocational, the chastity of other women is simply *per accidens* and *faute de mieux*; they are chaste in spite of themselves: '... the gallants of these times are shallow lechers, they put not their courtship home enough to a wench, 'tis impossible to know what woman is thoroughly honest, because she's ne'er thoroughly tried...' (II.i.297–300). 'Gentlemen, what is't you lack?' cries Mistress Openwork at the start of this scene. Laxton's name ('lack stone' ('stone' = 'testicle')) suggests one answer.

In this same scene Laxton, homoerotically attracted to the cross-dressed Moll and with the arrogance to assume she would welcome an assignation with him, waits until Moll has dispatched the armed 'Fellow' who has insulted her before safely voicing his willingness to fight:

---

[54] This edict is reported in a letter of John Chamberlain of 25 January 1620; quoted in Woodbridge, *Women and the English Renaissance*, p. 143.
[55] Mary Beth Rose, 'Women in Men's Clothes: Apparel and Social Stability in *The Roaring Girl*', *ELR*, 14 (1984), 377

LAXTON

Gallantly performed i'faith Moll, and manfully, I love thee forever
for't: base rogue, had he offered but the least counter-buff, by this
hand I was prepared for him.

MOLL

You prepared for him? Why should you be prepared for him, was he
any more than a man?   (II.i.243–7)

That last phrase, 'was he any more than a man?' succinctly under-
cuts the unmerited condescension of Laxton's 'manfully'.

'In a counterfeit world the truth should be dazzling.' So says
Moll in Nick Stafford's play *Moll Cutpurse*. Middleton and
Dekker's Moll *is* dazzling: 'as good marry a beacon on a hill', says
Sir Alexander to his son when he thinks him bent on marrying her
(II.ii.137). For all their common name there can be no confusion
between the play's two Molls. There is no call to exercise discernment in distinguishing between them as there is, for instance, in
distinguishing the False Florimell from the true in Edmund
Spenser's *Faerie Queene*. The very fact that Mary Frith had a real,
historical identity – an identity capable of visiting the theatre to
watch herself represented and perhaps stand in for the actor – sets
her apart from the others. As the play's true coin her role is that of
arbiter of value. It is against her truth that values are tested and
tried.

The authoritarian males, Sir Alexander and Sir Davy, make the
experientially sound patriarchal assumption that existing legislation
is on their side. They seek to use that law to further their own ends.
'I'll find law to hang her up' says Sir Alexander (I.ii.234); Sir Davy
sets Curtilax and Hanger – professional law-enforcers – on to his
son. In contrast to this appropriation of the legal status quo is the
self-legislation we encounter in the underworld, where laws and
legislators are of a more immediate, necessitous, and vital kind than
those to which Sir Alexander and Sir Davy apply. Here Moll is
supreme. Her assignations in III.i, first with Laxton and then with
Trapdoor, take place in Gray's Inn Fields, near the Inns of Court.
Laxton takes her to be 'some young barrister' (l.46) while
Trapdoor, jostled by the cross-dressed Moll, self-righteously hopes
'there's law for you, sir' (l.161). The setting focuses the contrast
between the patriarchal establishments of law and the kind of or-
ganic legislation that Moll operates in V.i, for example, when she
instructs a cutpurse to restore a purse which he stole from a knight
at the Swan (ll.288–90). Moll's supremacy as legislator comes by
virtue of her superior skill: a better fighter and more alert to the
reality around her than the others, she thereby wins their submis-
sion.

In much late Elizabethan and early Jacobean drama, virtue (the strength of goodness) is at odds with the more modern, Machiavellian, transitive *virtù* (the strength of being good *at it* – 'it' usually being some form of alert and duplicitous behaviour). In *King Lear* Edgar has virtue, Edmund *virtù*. In the figure of Moll, Middleton and Dekker – with little support from their biographical source – reidentified the two forms of virtue. Moll is both good and good at it.

Etymologically, 'virtue' and *virtù* are derived from the Latin *vir* = 'man'. 'Virtue' is cognate with 'virility' and is by nature strong.[56] But in *The Roaring Girl* it is Moll, not the bloodless 'hero' Sebastian, who actively embodies both. The almost magical powers of virginity had been celebrated in recent memory in the cult of Astraea surrounding Elizabeth I, the virgin queen.[57] Spenser's Britomart, female knight of Chastity, is active, resourceful, and armed. Moll's authority and her celibacy are linked: her self-legislation ('My spirit shall be mistress of this house, / As long as I have time in't' (III.i.139–40)) is the ground of her moral authority.

Her wonderful speech to Laxton in III.i (71–112) ferociously and with marvellous accuracy identifies those men who think 'each woman thy fond flexible whore, / If she but cast a liberal eye upon thee; / Turn back her head, she's thine'. The fineness of this speech stems only partly from her rich indignation at men who brag of non-existent sexual conquests. Her own authority to speak here is enhanced by her proud celibacy. But the speech also recognises that some women do indeed prostitute themselves:

> Distressed needlewomen and trade-fallen wives,
> Fish that must needs bite or themselves be bitten,
> Such hungry things as these may soon be took
> With a worm fastened on a golden hook:
> These are the lecher's food... (94–8)

She does not merely reject the application of the word 'whore' to herself, thereby validating the censure when correctly applied; she looks with realism and compassion at the situation of women who are driven to prostitution. Their poverty and vulnerability are the crimes, the exploiters of these the criminals. Though Moll is absolute in her own chastity, she witnesses a world in which there are worse wrongs than sexual incontinence.

Moll's role in Sebastian's plot is to signify all that a father like Sir Alexander could abhor in a daughter-in-law. All that Sebastian has

---

[56] The final couplet of Milton's masque *Comus*, 1634, admits of a possible separation: 'Or if Virtue feeble were, / Heaven itself would stoop to her.'

[57] See Frances A. Yates, *Astraea*, chapters 1 and 3.

to do in order to please his father is to marry 'not this' (V.ii.110). In the larger play, however, she provides a defining centre which *is* this. In Sir Alexander's final speech of contrition he casts 'the world's eyes from [him]' to look instead with his own and see what really is, in all its singularity. He forsakes the carelessness of consensual ideology which fails in discernment:

> I'll never more
> Condemn by common voice, for that's the whore
> That deceives man's opinion, mocks his trust,
> Cozens his love, and makes his heart unjust. (V.ii.248–51)

In more ways than one this is a play about justice.

THE SHARES OF THE TWO AUTHORS

The title-page of the quarto proclaims that *The Roaring Girl* was 'Written by T. Middleton and T. Dekkar'. Collaboration between playwrights at this period was common and several plays appear to have been written by a temporarily-grouped syndicate. Both Middleton and Dekker collaborated frequently with other writers: numerically speaking, collaboratively-written plays were the norm.[58] Attempts to allocate lines or scenes of the play to either Middleton or Dekker beg as many questions as they answer and have tended to be based on pre-existing valuations of each author.[59] The canting scene in V.i can be attributed to Dekker fairly confidently on account of its close correspondence with passages in his *Bellman of London* and *Lanthorn and Candlelight*. But the language of this scene and the world of cony-catching were not remote from Middleton. Of course, there are moments in the play when one feels one hears the 'authentic voice' of one of the two authors – a feeling based on familiarity with other, non-collaborative works. But all such attribution remains conjecture which may be confounded by the inextricable intimacy of the collaborative process. It appears that while on occasions the work of creation was divided

---

[58] See Neil Carson, *A Companion to Henslowe's Diary*, Cambridge, 1988, p. 57, where he states that in the spring and summer of 1598, 82 per cent of completed plays were written collaboratively.

[59] Fredson Bowers, editor of Dekker's *Dramatic Works*, assumes the play to be almost entirely Dekker's work, with the exception of 'a scene or two in which the authorship seems somewhat mixed' (Bowers, III, 8); Andor Gomme follows T. S. Eliot in thinking Dekker incapable of the creation of Moll (Gomme, p. xxxv); Mulholland (pp. 8–12) gives a detailed linguistic analysis of each scene and offers pointers to one author or the other but wisely refrains from allocating a governing responsibility to either.

between writers along fairly clear lines such as plot/execution, main plot/subplot, comic action/serious action, there are many instances where no such clear divisions exist.[60] Cyrus Hoy concludes: 'All that can be confidently said concerning the authorship of *The Roaring Girl* is that Dekker's unaided work is most apparent throughout the whole of Act I; in II.ii; and in V.i. Middleton's unaided work is most evident in II.i and III.i. For the rest (III.ii–iii; IV.i–ii; V.ii) the work of both dramatists is present in an admixture that I would not care to separate.'[61] Theatre is by its very nature the most collaborative of media. It is a mark of the play's success that its seams cannot be unpicked easily.

THE TEXT

The following note is largely the work of Andor Gomme, my predecessor in this series as editor of *The Roaring Girl*. I have checked his text against two copies of the first quarto of the play and made some silent corrections. In the few instances where my editorial decisions have involved a substantive variation from Gomme's text I have recorded this in the notes with my initials.

E.C.

The Roaring Girl was published by Thomas Archer in 1611 in the only early edition known; Archer did not enter it in the Stationers' Register.[62] Ten copies of the first quarto are known to have survived and are listed in Bowers's textual edition of the play.[63] The present text was prepared from a photographic reproduction of that in the Dyce Collection at the Victoria and Albert Museum, collated with one of two copies in the British Museum (Ashley 1159) and one in the Bodleian Library (Malone 246[1]). I have also used the text prepared by Professor Bowers, which notes all press-variants within the available copies of the quarto, as well as others noted below.

Most of these variants represent the correction of literals and minor amendments of punctuation which are of no significance.

---

[60] See S. Schoenbaum, *Internal Evidence and Elizabethan Dramatic Authorship*, Evanston, 1966, p. 226.

[61] Hoy, p. 12. His summary is based on the analyses of R. H. Barker (*Thomas Middleton*, p. 170) and Bullen (I, xxxvi).

[62] Bald's view (Chronology, p. 37), that the 'book concerning Mall Cutpurse' entered in the Stationers' Register by Ambrose Garland on 18 February 1612 may be *The Roaring Girl,* is really guesswork.

[63] See Bowers, III, 9, and W. W. Greg, *A Bibliography of the English Printed Drama to the Restoration*, London, 1939–50, p. 298.

Substantive changes occur only in signature I (1^v and 4$^{r\ \&\ v}$), i.e. IV.ii.51ff. and 223ff. The second of these involved resetting of type loosened when a forme was unlocked for a correction, but no verbal variants; those which occur in the first have no authority. A summary of the evidence of proof-correction is given in the textual introduction to Bowers's edition, which should be consulted for detailed information on variant-readings and accidentals, few of which are recorded in the notes to the present edition. All the few major cruces in the play are discussed briefly in the notes; the only one worth mentioning here is that which was responsible for the alterations at IV.ii.51 and 55. All copies of Q agree in having two consecutive speeches with the same prefix, the second occurrence of which is as the catchword at the bottom of a page. An attempt was apparently made during printing to correct this anomaly, but abandoned, though not without alterations working their way in.

The quarto was evidently printed from a carefully prepared manuscript, which Bowers and Price[64] believe to be Dekker's work, though it contains a number of contractions characteristic of Middleton. The transcription was either a fair copy made for the actors or derived from the prompt book – as might be suggested by the comprehensive but somewhat inconsistently worded and occasionally misaligned stage directions. Punctuation is variable and occasionally capricious, though generally – as in most of Middleton – light, with extensive use of commas where we might use heavier stops, which were indeed liberally provided by nineteenth-century editors. I have tried to preserve this lightness which seems appropriate for the racy conversational idiom in which so much of the play is written, while bringing some consistency to such matters as capitalisation and the use of question-marks (commonly omitted from Q, and where present often anticipating the end of the sentence). Some order has likewise been brought into common constructions which have, like the spelling, all been modernised, so that we read 'I'm' for 'Ime' or 'I'me', 'I'll' for 'Ile', 'You'd' for 'Youlde' and so on. I have kept 'Y'are' where it appears in the copy-text, for it implies a different pronunciation from 'You're', which in this edition where necessary replaces 'Your'. I have also made some attempt to relineate a few passages in which what seemed to me manifestly verse is printed as prose or, occasionally, vice versa. This is a task which must be approached with great caution, for Middleton's verse in particular is highly irregular, containing many lines of greater or less than normal length. Moreover, he moves easily from verse to a strongly rhythmical prose, and some

[64] George R. Price, 'The Manuscript and Quarto of *The Roaring Girl*', *The Library*, fifth series 11 (1956), 182–3

passages are in a mixture of the two: any attempt at wholesale regularisation of the verse is therefore to be avoided; nevertheless, it is clear that some of the irregularities are the result of compositorial endeavours to save or lose space, and it is misplaced piety to retain these. Asides are frequent, though rarely noted as such in Q: I have identified them where it seemed possible that readers might be misled, and have also supplied a few missing stage directions. There are no act and scene divisions in Q: this edition follows those established by Dyce, except that I agree with Bowers in dividing Act I into two scenes.

Since the first quarto, *The Roaring Girl* has appeared in Dodsley's *Select Collection of Old Plays* (1780), in Sir Walter Scott's *Ancient British Drama* (1810), vol. II, and, edited by J. P. Collier, in the third edition of Dodsley (1825). It was included in vol. II of Dyce's *Works of Thomas Middleton* (1840), the first to establish a canon. Bullen's edition of the *Works* (1885), in which *The Roaring Girl* appears in vol. IV, is based closely on Dyce; and Havelock Ellis's selection in the old Mermaid series (1887: *Roaring Girl* in vol. II) is virtually a reprint of parts of Bullen. A facsimile of one of the British Museum copies was issued by J. S. Farmer for the Tudor Facsimile Texts (1914). The full textual edition of Fredson Bowers appeared in 1958 in vol. III of *The Dramatic Works of Thomas Dekker*. Most recently it was edited by Paul A. Mulholland in 1987 for the Revels Plays.

FURTHER READING

Anon., *The Life and Death of Mrs. Mary Frith, commonly called Moll Cutpurse*, 1662, ed. Randall S. Nakayama, New York, 1993

R. C. Bald, 'The Sources of Middleton's City Comedies', *Journal of English and Germanic Philology*, 33 (1934), 373–87

R. H. Barker, *Thomas Middleton*, New York, 1958

Norman Berlin, 'Thomas Dekker: a Partial Reappraisal', *SEL*, 6 (1966), 273–5

M. C. Bradbrook, *The Growth and Structure of Elizabethan Comedy*, 2nd edn, Cambridge, 1973

Patrick Chenay, 'Moll Cutpurse as Hermaphrodite in Dekker and Middleton's *The Roaring Girl*', *Renaissance and Reformation*, new series 7 (old series 19) (1983), 120–34

Viviana Comensoli, 'Play-making, Domestic Conduct and the Multiple Plot in *The Roaring Girl*', *SEL*, 27 (1987), 249–66

M.-T. Jones Davies, *Un Peintre de la vie londonienne: Thomas Dekker*, 2 vols, Paris, 1958

Anthony B. Dawson, 'Mistress Hic and Haec: Representations of Moll Frith', *SEL*, 33 (1993), 385–404

Juliet Dusinberre, *Shakespeare and the Nature of Women*, London, 1975

T. S. Eliot, 'Thomas Middleton', in *Elizabethan Essays*, London, 1927, pp. 87–100

Una Ellis-Fermor, *The Jacobean Drama*, 4th edn, London, 1958

Dorothy M. Farr, *Thomas Middleton and the Drama of Realism*, Edinburgh, 1973

Ellen Galford, *Moll Cutpurse: Her True History*, 2nd edn, London, 1993

M. Garber, 'The Logic of the Transvestite in *The Roaring Girl*', in D. S. Kastan and P. Stallybrass (eds), *Staging the Renaissance: Reinterpretations of Elizabethan and Jacobean Drama*, London, 1991, pp. 221–34

Julia Gasper, *The Dragon and the Dove: The Plays of Thomas Dekker*, Oxford, 1990

Brian Gibbons, *Jacobean City Comedy*, 2nd edn, London, 1980

Margot Heinemann, *Puritanism and the Theatre: Thomas Middleton and Opposition Drama under the Early Stuarts*, Cambridge, 1980

Jean E. Howard, 'Cross-dressing, the Theater, and Gender Struggle in Early Modern England', in Lesley Ferris (ed.), *Crossing the Stage: Controversies on Cross-Dressing*, London, 1993, pp. 20–46

Mary Leland Hunt, *Thomas Dekker*, New York, 1911

G. K. Hunter, 'Bourgeois Comedy: Shakespeare and Dekker', in E. A. J. Honigmann (ed.), *Shakespeare and his Contemporaries: Essays in Comparison*, Manchester, 1986, pp. 1–15

Lisa Jardine, *Still Harping on Daughters: Women and Drama in the Age of Shakespeare*, 2nd edn, New York, 1983

L. C. Knights, *Drama and Society in the Age of Jonson*, London, 1937

Kathleen E. McLuskie, *Dekker and Heywood*, Basingstoke, 1994

E. H. Millar, 'Thomas Dekker, Hack Writer', *N&Q*, 200 (1955), 145–50

J. R. Mulryne, *Thomas Middleton*, Harlow, 1979

Stephen Orgel, 'The Subtexts of *The Roaring Girl*', in Susan Zimmerman (ed.), *Erotic Politics: Desire on the Renaissance Stage*, London, 1992, pp. 12–26

R. B. Parker, 'Middleton's Experiments with Comedy and Judgement', in J. R. Brown and B. Harris (eds), *Stratford-upon-Avon Studies 1, Jacobean Theatre*, London, 1960, 179–99

G. R. Price, *Thomas Dekker*, New York, 1969

Mary Beth Rose, 'Women in Men's Clothes: Apparel and Social Stability in *The Roaring Girl*,' *ELR*, 14 (1984), 367–91

S. Schoenbaum, '*A Chaste Maid in Cheapside* and Middleton's City Comedy', in J. W. Bennett et al. (eds), *Studies in English Renaissance Drama*, London, 1959, pp. 287–309

Simon Shepherd, *Amazons and Warrior Women: Varieties of Feminism in Seventeenth-Century Drama*, Brighton, 1981

Sara Jayne Steen, *Ambrosia in an Earthen Vessel: Three Centuries of Audience and Reader Response to the Works of Thomas Middleton*, New York, 1993

Susan Wells, 'Jacobean City Comedy and the Ideology of the City', *ELH*, 48 (1981), 37–60

Martin White, *Middleton and Tourneur*, Basingstoke, 1992

Linda Woodbridge, *Women and the English Renaissance: Literature and the Nature of Womankind 1540–1620*, Brighton, 1984

The Fortune-stage See above, pp. xxiii–xxv.

The Prince his Players In 1603 the Admiral's Men, who had for over twenty years been the servants of Lord Howard of Effingham, Lord High Admiral, were transferred to Prince Henry, James I's eldest son. Three years before, they had made the Fortune their permanent home under the lucrative but somewhat tyrannical overlordship of Edward Alleyn and Philip Henslowe, whose diary (up to 1603) provides copious notes of the company's activities.

Popes head-pallace The Pope's Head Tavern in Pope's Head Alley (a lane running south from Cornhill to Lombard Street) may have been originally part of King John's palace. More than one bookseller is recorded as issuing books from the 'Palace', and the alley was largely occupied by booksellers' shops from about 1600. Thomas Archer was also the printer in 1609 of the anonymous *Every Woman in Her Humour*.

My case is alter'd, I must worke for my liuing The first half of the sentence is a common proverbial expression, giving title to one of Jonson's comedies (1597, published 1609). The whole sentence may be a quotation; 'case' in this context refers to clothing. Moll (i.e. Mary Frith) is shown in the picture wearing 'the great Dutch slop' (see II.ii.81–2); she has a 'standing collar' (III.iii.28) and 'roses' on her shoes (IV.ii.7).

The Roaring Girle.

OR
Moll Cut-Purse.

As it hath lately beene Acted on the Fortune-stage by
the Prince his Players.

Written by *T. Middleton* and *T. Dekkar*.

My case is alter'd, I must worke for my liuing.

Printed at *London* for *Thomas Archer*, and are to be fold at his
fhop in Popes head-pallace, neere the Royall
Exchange. 1611.

TO THE COMIC PLAY-READERS, VENERY AND LAUGHTER

The fashion of play-making I can properly compare to nothing so naturally as the alteration in apparel: for in the time of the great crop-doublet, your huge bombasted plays, quilted with mighty words to lean purpose, was only then in fashion. And as the doublet fell, neater inventions began to 5
set up. Now in the time of spruceness, our plays follow the niceness of our garments, single plots, quaint conceits, lecherous jests, dressed up in hanging sleeves, and those are fit for the times and the termers: such a kind of light-colour summer stuff, mingled with diverse colours, you shall find this pub- 10
lished comedy, good to keep you in an afternoon from dice, at home in your chambers; and for venery you shall find enough for sixpence, but well couched and you mark it. For Venus being a woman passes through the play in doublet and breeches, a brave disguise and a safe one, if the statute untie 15
not her codpiece point. The book I make no question but is fit for many of your companies, as well as the person itself,

---

Title *Venery* good hunting, or (in this play more importantly) the pursuit of sexual pleasure. Cf. III.i.41 and *Northward Ho!*, III.i.87: 'Venery is like usury ... it may be allowed though it be not lawful.'

3 *crop-doublet* a short doublet, richly padded, which went out of fashion about 1580. Stubbes in his *Anatomy of Abuses* (1583) writes of 'doublets with great bellies ... stuffed with four, five, or six pounds of bombast at the least'. Bombast was cotton wool used for stuffing, but the word was regularly in figurative use as well.

5 *as the doublet fell* It became longer and longer till the 1590s, but then shrank and became hollow-bellied.

7 *single plots* hardly characteristic of 1611, and Middleton may be writing ironically

8 *hanging sleeves* no longer caught in at the cuff

9 *termers* those who came to London for the terms of the Inns of Court, often just for amusement

13 *sixpence* the ordinary price of a (printed) play
well couched both 'richly embroidered' and 'well hidden'
and an (=if)

15–16 *if the statute untie not her codpiece point* Though there was much legislation regulating the dress of particular trades and classes, none is known which proscribed women from wearing men's clothes. Presumably, therefore, the phrase is proleptic: 'provided no law is made to prevent her going dressed as a man'. Points were tags used to tie breeches or doublet (see III.i.59–60).

2

and may be allowed both gallery room at the playhouse, and
chamber room at your lodging. Worse things I must needs
confess the world has taxed her for, than has been written of   20
her; but 'tis the excellency of a writer to leave things better
than he finds 'em; though some obscene fellow (that cares not
what he writes against others, yet keeps a mystical bawdy-
house himself, and entertains drunkards to make use of their
pockets and vent his private bottle-ale at midnight) – though   25
such a one would have ripped up the most nasty vice that ever
hell belched forth, and presented it to a modest assembly, yet
we rather wish in such discoveries, where reputation lies
bleeding, a slackness of truth, than a fullness of slander.

THOMAS MIDDLETON

18 *gallery room* The tiring room at the Fortune was an enclosed continuation of the
   upper gallery; presumably copies of plays were kept here.
19 *Worse things* For what had been written of Moll Cutpurse see above, pp. xix–xxii.
22 *obscene* loathsome
23 *mystical* secret, unavowed
25 *vent his private bottle-ale* There seems almost certainly some sexual joke here, but
   I cannot reconstruct it. 'Bottle-ale' appears in *2 Henry IV*, II.iv.131, where the
   Arden editor suggests it means small beer; and this seems to be confirmed by a
   remark in Nashe's *Fouleweather's Prognostications* (*Works*, ed. Wilson, III, 392):
   'the predominant qualities of this [the summer] quarter is heat and dryness,
   whereby I do gather that, through the influence of Cancer, bottle-ale shall be in
   great authority, and wheat shall do knights' service unto malt. Tapsters this
   quarter shall be in greater credit than cobblers, and many shall drink more than
   they can earn.' But it could also mean simply windy rhetoric (see Marston,
   Histriomastix, III.i.202); 'vent' can mean sniff out, uncover, or emit (urine, wind,
   etc.), and 'bottle' was one of innumerable words for the female pudenda (cf.
   Measure for Measure, III.ii.172).
26 *ripped up* brought into the open

DRAMATIS PERSONAE

SIR ALEXANDER WENGRAVE, *and* NEATFOOT *his man*
SIR ADAM APPLETON
SIR DAVY DAPPER
SIR BEAUTEOUS GANYMEDE
[SIR THOMAS LONG]   5
LORD NOLAND
Young [SEBASTIAN] WENGRAVE
JACK DAPPER, *and* GULL *his page*
GOSHAWK
GREENWIT   10
LAXTON

TILTYARD [*a feather-seller*] ⎤
OPENWORK [*a sempster*]   ⎬ *Cives & Uxores*
GALLIPOT [*an apothecary*]   ⎦

MOLL *the Roaring Girl*   15
TRAPDOOR
[TEARCAT]

SIR GUY FITZ-ALLARD
MARY FITZ-ALLARD *his daughter*

CURTILAX *a Sergeant, and*   20
HANGER *his Yeoman*

Ministri

[*Coachman, Porter, Tailor, Gentlemen, Cutpurses, Fellow*]

1, 7 WENGRAVE ed. (Wentgraue Q)   1 NEATFOOT ed. (Neats-foot Q)
12 TILTYARD The word means a tilting or jousting ground: its aptness for a feather-
   seller possibly lies in the link between feathers and archery, or feathers and gallants. The sense of 'yard' as 'penis' is also played upon.
12–14 *Cives & Uxores* (Lat.) Citizens and their Wives
13 OPENWORK Work made like lace or crochet to show a pattern of holes. His name
   also reflects his nature.
14 GALLIPOT A small glazed earthenware jar, especially one used for medicines, and
   hence a jocular name for an apothecary. Cf. also *The Honest Whore*, part 2,
   I.ii.139: '[A harlot] is the Gally-pot to which these Drones flye, not for love to
   the pot, but for the sweet sucket within it, her money, her money.'
22 *Ministri* (Lat.) Servants

PROLOGUS

A play expected long makes the audience look
For wonders: – that each scene should be a book,
Composed to all perfection; each one comes
And brings a play in's head with him: up he sums
What he would of a roaring girl have writ;   5
If that he finds not here, he mews at it.
Only we entreat you think our scene
Cannot speak high (the subject being but mean);
A roaring girl, whose notes till now never were,
Shall fill with laughter our vast theatre,   10
That's all which I dare promise: tragic passion,
And such grave stuff, is this day out of fashion.
I see attention sets wide ope her gates
Of hearing, and with covetous listening waits,
To know what girl this roaring girl should be.   15
For of that tribe are many: one is she
That roars at midnight in deep tavern bowls,
That beats the watch, and constables controls;
Another roars i'th'daytime, swears, stabs, gives braves,
Yet sells her soul to the lust of fools and slaves.   20
Both these are suburb-roarers. Then there's beside
A civil city-roaring girl, whose pride,
Feasting, and riding, shakes her husband's state,
And leaves him roaring through an iron grate.
None of these roaring girls is ours: she flies   25
With wings more lofty. Thus her character lies,
Yet what need characters, when to give a guess
Is better than the person to express?
But would you know who 'tis? Would you hear her name?
She is called Mad Moll; her life our acts proclaim.   30

6 *mews* jeers by mewing
10 *our vast theatre* The Fortune was a large theatre, though not excessively so: see
  p. xxiii.
14 *covetous* eager
18 *beats the watch* knocks the watchman about. The watch were in the charge of a
  constable; the forerunners of the police, they stayed awake at night to keep
  watch, and were often portrayed as comical and incompetent (as in *Much Ado
  About Nothing*).
19 *gives braves* offers battle
21 *suburb-roarers* lower-class, with a dig at the proverbially licentious character of
  London suburbs. Cf. V.ii.25 and note.
  beside ed. (besides Q)
24 *through an iron grate* i.e. in prison

THE ROARING GIRL

Act I, Scene i

Enter MARY FITZ-ALLARD *disguised like a sempster with a
case for bands, and* NEATFOOT *a serving-man with her,
with a napkin on his shoulder and a trencher in his hand,
as from table*

NEATFOOT

The young gentleman, our young master, Sir Alexander's
son, is it into his ears, sweet damsel, emblem of fragility,
you desire to have a message transported, or to be transcendent?

MARY

A private word or two, sir, nothing else.   5

NEATFOOT

You shall fructify in that which you come for: your pleasure shall be satisfied to your full contentation: I will,
fairest tree of generation, watch when our young master is
erected, that is to say, up, and deliver him to this your
most white hand.   10

MARY

Thanks, sir.

NEATFOOT

And withal certify him, that I have culled out for him, now
his belly is replenished, a daintier bit or modicum than any
lay upon his trencher at dinner. Hath he notion of your
name, I beseech your chastity?   15

MARY

One, sir, of whom he bespake falling bands.

NEATFOOT

Falling bands, it shall so be given him. – If you please to

---

0 sd 1 *sempster* The form of the word, now restricted to the masculine, was originally, like all *-ster* forms, feminine.

0 sd 1–2 *a case for bands* a box for holding collar-bands

3 *transcendent* Unless the word has an unidentified obscene meaning, Neatfoot
   must mean it to imply a private colloquy between Mary and Sebastian, but his
   language is of course deliberately affected. Cf. Osric (*Hamlet*, V.ii) and, for a
   closer parallel, Dondolo (*Revenger's Tragedy*, II.i).

16 *falling bands* bands worn falling flat round the neck (said by Evelyn to be a new
    mode in 1625)

venture your modesty in the hall, amongst a curl-pated
company of rude serving-men, and take such as they can
set before you, you shall be most seriously, and ingeni-   20
ously welcome.

MARY

I have dined indeed already, sir.

NEATFOOT

Or will you vouchsafe to kiss the lip of a cup of rich
Orleans in the buttery amongst our waiting-women?

MARY

Not now in truth, sir.   25

NEATFOOT

Our young master shall then have a feeling of your being
here: presently it shall so be given him.   *Exit*

MARY

I humbly thank you, sir. But that my bosom
Is full of bitter sorrows, I could smile
To see this formal ape play antic tricks: 30
But in my breast a poisoned arrow sticks,
And smiles cannot become me. Love woven slightly
(Such as thy false heart makes) wears out as lightly,
But love being truly bred i'th'soul (like mine)
Bleeds even to death, at the least wound it takes: 35
The more we quench this fire, the less it slakes.
Oh me!

Enter SEBASTIAN WENGRAVE *with* NEATFOOT

SEBASTIAN

A sempster speak with me, sayest thou?

NEATFOOT

Yes sir, she's there, *viva voce*, to deliver her auricular confession.   40

---

18 *curl-pated* Curling the hair was much affected at this time: Macaulay speaks of
   the curl-pated minions of James I.
20–1 *ingeniously* ingenuously (the two words were often confused)
22 *dined* ed. (dyed Q)
24 *Orleans* wine from the Loire area, often referred to in contemporary plays
33 *thy* (stet Q). Perhaps we should read 'the', which would confirm the proverbial
   character of Mary's observations; but she may be making a direct complaint of
   Sebastian.
36 *fire* ed. (Q omits)
39–40 *viva voce* (Lat.) with living voice; i.e. in person
   auricular confession The phrase was normally used of confession to a priest, and
   hence implied suspicion of something treasonable. 'Confession' frequently had
   sexual overtones.

SEBASTIAN
With me, sweetheart? What is't?
MARY
I have brought home your bands, sir.
SEBASTIAN
Bands? – Neatfoot.
NEATFOOT
Sir.
SEBASTIAN
Prithee look in, for all the gentlemen are upon rising.   45
NEATFOOT
Yes sir, a most methodical attendance shall be given.
SEBASTIAN
And dost hear? If my father call for me, say I am busy with
a sempster.
NEATFOOT
Yes sir, he shall know it that you are busied with a needle-
woman.   50
SEBASTIAN
In's ear, good Neatfoot.
NEATFOOT
It shall be so given him.   *Exit*
SEBASTIAN
Bands? Y'are mistaken, sweetheart, I bespake none: when,
where, I prithee? What bands? Let me see them.
MARY
Yes sir, a bond fast sealed, with solemn oaths,   55
Subscribed unto (as I thought) with your soul,
Delivered as your deed in sight of heaven:
Is this bond cancelled, have you forgot me?
SEBASTIAN
Ha! Life of my life, Sir Guy Fitz-Allard's daughter,
What has transformed my love to this strange shape?   60
Stay: make all sure. – So: now speak and be brief,
Because the wolf's at door that lies in wait
To prey upon us both. Albeit mine eyes

---

42 *bands* neckbands i.e. ruffs or collars. At least that is what Sebastian takes the
'sempster' to mean.
49–50 *needlewoman* A cant word for a harlot, 'expert with pricks': this brings to a
climax Neatfoot's obscene punning which I take to be so broad earlier in the
scene as not to need special identification.
55 *bond* 'Bond' and 'band' were used interchangeably in the figurative senses.
62 *the wolf's at door* 'To keep the wolf from the door' was proverbial from an early
date: cf. Skelton, *Colin Clout*, 146ff., 'some there be ... Like Aaron and Ure, /
The wolf from the door / To werrin and to keep / From their ghostly sheep'.

Are blessed by thine, yet this so strange disguise
Holds me with fear and wonder.
MARY   Mine's a loathed sight,   65
Why from it are you banished else so long?
SEBASTIAN
I must cut short my speech: in broken language,
Thus much: sweet Moll, I must thy company shun,
I court another Moll, my thoughts must run
As a horse runs that's blind, round in a mill,   70
Out every step, yet keeping one path still.
MARY
Hm! Must you shun my company? In one knot
Have both our hands by th'hands of heaven been tied,
Now to be broke? I thought me once your bride:
Our fathers did agree on the time when: 75
And must another bedfellow fill my room?
SEBASTIAN
Sweet maid, let's lose no time: 'tis in heaven's book
Set down, that I must have thee: an oath we took
To keep our vows; but when the knight your father
Was from mine parted, storms began to sit   80
Upon my covetous father's brows, which fell
From them on me: he reckoned up what gold
This marriage would draw from him, at which he swore,
To lose so much blood could not grieve him more.
He then dissuades me from thee, called thee not fair,   85
And asked what is she but a beggar's heir?
He scorned thy dowry of five thousand marks.
If such a sum of money could be found,
And I would match with that, he'd not undo it,
Provided his bags might add nothing to it,   90
But vowed, if I took thee, nay more, did swear it,
Save birth, from him I nothing should inherit.
MARY
What follows then, my shipwreck?

---

70 *As a horse ... in a mill* The horse used to turn small millstones walked in a constant circle round the stone; hence (in the next line), Sebastian's thoughts are
away from their proper place, yet always keeping to the one path. The phrase
was proverbial and used elsewhere by Dekker: cf. *Northward Ho!*, I.iii.129: 'I
that like a horse / Ran blindfold in a mill (all in one circle).'
81 *brows* ed. (E.C.) (brow Q)
87 *five thousand marks* This was a lot of money (£3,333) and well above the aver-
age marriage settlement among the gentry. See Mulholland, p. 58 n. 65.

SEBASTIAN   Dearest, no:
  Though wildly in a labyrinth I go,
  My end is to meet thee: with a side wind   95
  Must I now sail, else I no haven can find,
  But both must sink forever. There's a wench
  Called Moll, mad Moll, or merry Moll, a creature
  So strange in quality, a whole city takes
  Note of her name and person: all that affection   100
  I owe to thee, on her in counterfeit passion
  I spend to mad my father: he believes
  I doat upon this roaring girl, and grieves
  As it becomes a father for a son
  That could be so bewitched: yet I'll go on   105
  This crooked way, sigh still for her, feign dreams
  In which I'll talk only of her: these streams
  Shall, I hope, force my father to consent
  That here I anchor, rather than be rent
  Upon a rock so dangerous. Art thou pleased,   110
  Because thou seest we are waylaid, that I take
  A path that's safe, though it be far about?
MARY
  My prayers with heaven guide thee!
SEBASTIAN   Then I will on.
  My father is at hand, kiss and begone;
  Hours shall be watched for meetings; I must now,   115
  As men for fear, to a strange idol bow.
MARY
  Farewell.
SEBASTIAN   I'll guide thee forth: when next we meet,
  A story of Moll shall make our mirth more sweet.   *Exeunt*

[Act I, Scene ii]

Enter SIR ALEXANDER WENGRAVE, SIR DAVY DAPPER,
SIR ADAM APPLETON, GOSHAWK, LAXTON, and
GENTLEMEN

OMNES
  Thanks, good Sir Alexander, for our bounteous cheer.
SIR ALEXANDER
  Fie, fie, in giving thanks you pay too dear.

102 *to mad* a transitive verb; 'madden'

  1 sp OMNES (Lat.) All

SIR DAVY
> When bounty spreads the table, faith 'twere sin,
> At going off, if thanks should not step in.

SIR ALEXANDER
> No more of thanks, no more: ay, marry sir.   5
> Th'inner room was too close, how do you like
> This parlour, gentlemen?

OMNES   Oh passing well.

SIR ADAM
> What a sweet breath the air casts here, so cool!

GOSHAWK
> I like the prospect best.

LAXTON   See how 'tis furnished.

SIR DAVY
> A very fair sweet room.

SIR ALEXANDER   Sir Davy Dapper,   10
> The furniture that doth adorn this room
> Cost many a fair grey groat ere it came here,
> But good things are most cheap, when th'are most dear.
> Nay when you look into my galleries,
> How bravely they are trimmed up, you all shall swear   15
> Y'are highly pleased to see what's set down there:
> Stories of men and women, mixed together
> Fair ones with foul, like sunshine in wet weather;
> Within one square a thousand heads are laid
> So close that all of heads the room seems made;   20
> As many faces there, filled with blithe looks,
> Show like the promising titles of new books
> Writ merrily, the readers being their own eyes,
> Which seem to move and to give plaudities;
> And here and there, whilst with obsequious ears   25

11–32 These lines may describe the Fortune. See above, pp. xxii–xxv.

12 *grey groat* The phrase is commonly an emphatic to suggest something of little value, but here perhaps means of silver.

13 *good things ... dear* A version of a popular saying recorded by Tilley in several forms, e.g., 'Good cheap is dear' and 'The dearer it is the cheaper' (M. P. Tilley, *A Dictionary of Proverbs in England in the Sixteenth and Seventeenth Centuries*, Ann Arbor, 1950)

14ff. Sir Alexander's collection suggests a parody of the great collections which began to be made in Elizabeth's reign, and of which Lord Lumley's at Nonsuch Palace, Surrey, was an already famous example. Pictures were sometimes fixed to the wall so close together as to make a mosaic covering the wall entirely. The display hints at the kind of spectacular stage effects which were then becoming popular in masques and is a kind of visual diagram of the action of the play.

24 *plaudities* rounds of applause

Thronged heaps do listen, a cutpurse thrusts and leers
With hawk's eyes for his prey: I need not show him,
By a hanging villainous look yourselves may know him,
The face is drawn so rarely. Then sir, below,
The very floor, as 'twere, waves to and fro,   30
And like a floating island seems to move,
Upon a sea bound in with shores above.

Enter SEBASTIAN *and* M[ASTER] GREENWIT

OMNES
These sights are excellent.
SIR ALEXANDER   I'll show you all:
Since we are met, make our parting comical.
SEBASTIAN
This gentleman, my friend, will take his leave, sir.   35
SIR ALEXANDER
Ha, take his leave, Sebastian? Who?
SEBASTIAN   This gentleman.
SIR ALEXANDER
Your love, sir, has already given me some time,
And if you please to trust my age with more,
It shall pay double interest: good sir, stay.
GREENWIT
I have been too bold.
SIR ALEXANDER   Not so, sir. A merry day   40
'Mongst friends being spent, is better than gold saved.
Some wine, some wine. Where be these knaves I keep?

Enter three or four SERVING-MEN, *and* NEATFOOT

NEATFOOT
At your worshipful elbow, sir.
SIR ALEXANDER
You are kissing my maids, drinking, or fast asleep.
NEATFOOT
Your worship has given it us right.

---

31 *a floating island* A *trompe-l'oeil* effect must be in mind here, intended to draw the audience more completely into the spectacle. Dekker picks up the idea again in *The Wonder of a Kingdom* (III.i.16ff.) and takes the parody further: 'I'll pave my great hall with a floor of clouds, / Wherein shall move an artificial sun, / Reflecting round about me golden beams / Whose flames shall make the room seem all on fire...' All the devices are to give an image of the world turned upside down.

34 *comical* happy, cheerful

40–1 *A merry day ... gold saved* This sounds proverbial, but is not recorded in Tilley's or Whiting's dictionaries of proverbs.

SIR ALEXANDER   You varlets, stir: 45
  Chairs, stools, and cushions: prithee Sir Davy Dapper,
  Make that chair thine.
SIR DAVY   'Tis but an easy gift,
  And yet I thank you for it, sir, I'll take it.
SIR ALEXANDER
  A chair for old Sir Adam Appleton.
NEATFOOT
  A back friend to your worship.
SIR ADAM   Marry, good Neatfoot,   50
  I thank thee for it: back friends sometimes are good.
SIR ALEXANDER
  Pray make that stool your perch, good Master Goshawk.
GOSHAWK
  I stoop to your lure, sir.
SIR ALEXANDER   Son Sebastian,
  Take Master Greenwit to you.
SEBASTIAN   Sit, dear friend.
SIR ALEXANDER
  Nay Master Laxton – furnish Master Laxton   55
  With what he wants, a stone – a stool I would say,
  A stool.
LAXTON   I had rather stand, sir.
SIR ALEXANDER   I know you had,
  Good Master Laxton. So, so.

Exeunt [NEATFOOT *and*] SERVANTS

Now here's a mess of friends, and, gentlemen,
Because time's glass shall not be running long,   60

---

50 *back friend* A backer (in this instance, the back of a chair), but playing on the
  alternative meaning of false friend. At this period stools were still commoner
  than chairs even in fairly elegant houses.
52 *Master* ed. (M. Q)
53 *stoop* submit (a technical term); *lure* falconer's apparatus for recalling a hawk.
  The terminology plays on Goshawk's name.
56–8 lineation ed. (With what ... stool / I had ... stand sir. / I know ... So, so Q)
56–7 *what he wants ... stand* A weak quibble on Laxton's name (he lacks a stone)
  becomes an insulting jibe when one remembers that 'stone' was standard
  English for testicle. (Cf. the assumed name Singlestone in *A Mad World, My
  Masters*, II.vi.26, which plainly suggests eunuch.) To 'stand' had various sexual
  meanings, here especially to have an erection; to stand to a woman is to prepare
  for intercourse, and a stallion is said to stand at stud.
58 sd here ed. (at 57 Q): *So, so* appears to be a gesture of dismissal to the servants.
59 *mess* company eating together
60 *Because ... long* so that time should not hang heavy on us

I'll quicken it with a pretty tale.

SIR DAVY   Good tales do well
In these bad days, where vice does so excel.

SIR ADAM
Begin, Sir Alexander.

SIR ALEXANDER   Last day I met
An aged man upon whose head was scored
A debt of just so many years as these   65
Which I owe to my grave: the man you all know.

OMNES
His name I pray you, sir.

SIR ALEXANDER   Nay, you shall pardon me:
But when he saw me, with a sigh that brake,
Or seemed to break, his heart-strings, thus he spake:
Oh my good knight, says he (and then his eyes   70
Were richer even by that which made them poor,
They had spent so many tears they had no more),
Oh sir, says he, you know it, for you ha' seen
Blessings to rain upon mine house and me:
Fortune, who slaves men, was my slave: her wheel   75
Hath spun me golden threads, for, I thank heaven,
I ne'er had but one cause to curse my stars.
I asked him then what that one cause might be.

OMNES
So, sir?

SIR ALEXANDER He paused; and as we often see
A sea so much becalmed there can be found   80
No wrinkle on his brow, his waves being drowned
In their own rage: but when th'imperious winds
Use strange invisible tyranny to shake
Both heaven's and earth's foundation at their noise,
The seas, swelling with wrath to part that fray,   85
Rise up, and are more wild, more mad than they –
Even so, this good old man was by my question
Stirred up to roughness, you might see his gall
Flow even in's eyes: then grew he fantastical.

SIR DAVY
Fantastical? Ha, ha.

SIR ALEXANDER   Yes, and talked oddly.   90

82 *winds* ed. (wind Q)
85 *part that fray* i.e. that caused by the winds: grammar and syntax are jumbled and
   inconsequent in this passage
86 *they* i.e. the winds
90 *talked* ed. (talk Q, talkt Dyce)

SIR ADAM
    Pray sir, proceed,
    How did this old man end?
SIR ALEXANDER   Marry sir, thus.
    He left his wild fit to read o'er his cards:
    Yet then (though age cast snow on all his hairs)
    He joyed because, says he, the god of gold   95
    Has been to me no niggard: that disease
    Of which all old men sicken, avarice,
    Never infected me –
LAXTON
    [*Aside*] He means not himself, I'm sure.
SIR ALEXANDER   For like a lamp
    Fed with continual oil, I spend and throw   100
    My light to all that need it, yet have still
    Enough to serve myself: oh but, quoth he,
    Though heaven's dew fall thus on this aged tree,
    I have a son that's like a wedge doth cleave
    My very heart-root.
SIR DAVY   Had he such a son?   105
SEBASTIAN
    [*Aside*] Now I do smell a fox strongly.
SIR ALEXANDER
    Let's see: no, Master Greenwit is not yet
    So mellow in years as he; but as like Sebastian,
    Just like my son Sebastian, such another.
SEBASTIAN
    [*Aside*] How finely, like a fencer, my father fetches his by- 110
    blows to hit me, but if I beat you not at your own weapon
    of subtlety –
SIR ALEXANDER
    This son, saith he, that should be
    The column and main arch unto my house,
    The crutch unto my age, becomes a whirlwind   115
    Shaking the firm foundation –
SIR ADAM   'Tis some prodigal.

---

93 *read o'er his cards* (stet Q): reckon up his position; Bowers emends to 'cares'
98–9 The aside interrupts the complete line which is spoken aloud.
110–11 *by-blows* strokes from the side
114 *The column ... unto my house* Cf. Tourneur, *The Atheist's Tragedy*, V.i.78f.: 'On
    these two pillars [his sons] stood the stately frame / And architecture of my lofty
    house.'

SEBASTIAN
[*Aside*] Well shot, old Adam Bell.
SIR ALEXANDER
No city monster neither, no prodigal,
But sparing, wary, civil, and (though wifeless)
An excellent husband, and such a traveller,   120
He has more tongues in his head than some have teeth.
SIR DAVY
I have but two in mine.
GOSHAWK
So sparing and so wary?
What then could vex his father so?
SIR ALEXANDER   Oh, a woman.
SEBASTIAN
A flesh-fly, that can vex any man.
SIR ALEXANDER   A scurvy woman,   125
On whom the passionate old man swore he doated:
A creature, saith he, nature hath brought forth
To mock the sex of woman. It is a thing
One knows not how to name: her birth began
Ere she was all made: 'tis woman more than man,   130
Man more than woman, and (which to none can hap)
The sun gives her two shadows to one shape:
Nay more, let this strange thing walk, stand or sit,
No blazing star draws more eyes after it.

---

117 *Adam Bell* the famous archer who figures in the ballad of *Adam Bell, Clym of the Clough and William of Cloudesley*

121 *more tongues . . . teeth* This presumably alludes to Sebastian's knowledge of languages; but proverbial phrases about the tongue usually had another edge to them. 'Double-tongued' meant deceitful (see II.ii.10n.) and cf. 'The tongue walks where the teeth speed not', a proverb quoted by Dekker in *The Gull's Horn-Book*, v.

125 *flesh-fly* literally, a fly which deposits its eggs in dead flesh

128ff. This passage was taken over by Field into the Mall Cutpurse scene in *Amends for Ladies* (II.i.33ff.): see above, p. xxi.

132 *two shadows to one shape* The implication is perhaps that by witchcraft she has stolen a shadow and so would have power over another's soul. The devil was normally held to cast no shadow. Possibly Sir Alexander also suggests that she has one shadow for a man and one for a woman.

134 *blazing star* i.e. a meteor, held in Elizabethan cosmology to be of ill omen, as belonging to the sublunary world of change and decay, as opposed to stars which were considered to be pure, fixed, and eternal. Cf. *The Changeling* (ed. Bawcutt, 1958), V.iii.154–5 and n.; and below, III.ii.98 and n. Bald (Chronology, p. 38) suggests that the comparison may have been prompted by the presence of Halley's comet.

SIR DAVY
A monster, 'tis some monster.
SIR ALEXANDER   She's a varlet.   135
SEBASTIAN
[*Aside*] Now is my cue to bristle.
SIR ALEXANDER
A naughty pack.
SEBASTIAN   'Tis false.
SIR ALEXANDER   Ha, boy?
SEBASTIAN   'Tis false.
SIR ALEXANDER
What's false? I say she's naught.
SEBASTIAN   I say that tongue
That dares speak so, but yours, sticks in the throat
Of a rank villain: set yourself aside –   140
SIR ALEXANDER
So sir, what then?
SEBASTIAN   Any here else had lied.
(*Aside*) I think I shall fit you.
SIR ALEXANDER
Lie?
SEBASTIAN Yes.
SIR DAVY   Doth this concern him?
SIR ALEXANDER   [*Aside*] Ah sirrah boy,
Is your blood heated? Boils it? Are you stung?
I'll pierce you deeper yet. – Oh my dear friends,   145
I am that wretched father, this that son,
That sees his ruin, yet headlong on doth run.
SIR ADAM
Will you love such a poison?
SIR DAVY   Fie, fie.
SEBASTIAN   Y'are all mad.
SIR ALEXANDER
Th'art sick at heart, yet feel'st it not: of all these,
What gentleman but thou, knowing his disease   150
Mortal, would shun the cure? Oh Master Greenwit,
Would you to such an idol bow?
GREENWIT   Not I, sir.
SIR ALEXANDER
Here's Master Laxton, has he mind to a woman

---

137 *naughty pack* person of low or worthless character (cf. the still current 'baggage')
142 sd (*Aside*) This stands in Q in roman type at the end of the line after a dash, evi-
     dently influenced by the spoken word 'aside' two lines above
     fit have something ready for

As thou hast?

LAXTON   No, not I, sir.

SIR ALEXANDER   Sir, I know it.

LAXTON
Their good parts are so rare, their bad so common,   155
I will have nought to do with any woman.

SIR DAVY
'Tis well done, Master Laxton.

SIR ALEXANDER   Oh thou cruel boy,
Thou would'st with lust an old man's life destroy;
Because thou see'st I'm half-way in my grave,
Thou shovel'st dust upon me: would thou might'st have 160
Thy wish, most wicked, most unnatural!

SIR DAVY
Why sir, 'tis thought Sir Guy Fitz-Allard's daughter
Shall wed your son Sebastian.

SIR ALEXANDER   Sir Davy Dapper,
I have upon my knees wooed this fond boy
To take that virtuous maiden.

SEBASTIAN   Hark you a word, sir.   165
You on your knees have cursed that virtuous maiden,
And me for loving her, yet do you now
Thus baffle me to my face? Wear not your knees
In such entreats, give me Fitz-Allard's daughter.

SIR ALEXANDER
I'll give thee rats-bane rather.

SEBASTIAN   Well then you know   170
What dish I mean to feed upon.

SIR ALEXANDER
Hark gentlemen, he swears
To have this cutpurse drab, to spite my gall.

OMNES
Master Sebastian –

SEBASTIAN   I am deaf to you all.
I'm so bewitched, so bound to my desires,   175
Tears, prayers, threats, nothing can quench out those fires
That burn within me.   *Exit*

SIR ALEXANDER [*Aside*]   Her blood shall quench it then.
– Lose him not, oh dissuade him, gentlemen.

155 *Their ... their* ed. (There ... there Q)
156 *nought* There is a contradictory play on 'naught' (as in 'naughty').
168 *baffle* hoodwink, contradict; perhaps with a secondary meaning of disgrace
    Wear ed. (were Q)
176 *quench out* (stet Q): perhaps we should omit 'out', for better scansion and for a
    more exact parallel with the following line.

SIR DAVY
He shall be weaned, I warrant you.
SIR ALEXANDER   Before his eyes
Lay down his shame, my grief, his miseries.   180
OMNES   No more, no more, away.

Exeunt all but SIR ALEXANDER

SIR ALEXANDER   I wash a negro,
Losing both pains and cost: but take thy flight,
I'll be most near thee when I'm least in sight.
Wild buck, I'll hunt thee breathless, thou shalt run on,
But I will turn thee when I'm not thought upon.   185

Enter RALPH TRAPDOOR

Now sirrah, what are you? Leave your ape's tricks and
speak.
TRAPDOOR
A letter from my captain to your worship.
SIR ALEXANDER
Oh, oh, now I remember, 'tis to prefer thee into my ser-
vice.   190
TRAPDOOR
To be a shifter under your worship's nose of a clean
trencher, when there's a good bit upon't.
SIR ALEXANDER
Troth, honest fellow – [*Aside*] Hm – ha – let me see,
This knave shall be the axe to hew that down
At which I stumble, 'has a face that promiseth   195
Much of a villain: I will grind his wit,
And if the edge prove fine make use of it.
– Come hither sirrah, canst thou be secret, ha?
TRAPDOOR
As two crafty attorneys plotting the undoing of their
clients.   200

---

181 *I wash a negro* 'To wash an Ethiop (or blackamoor) white' is a common
   proverbial expression first recorded in late classical times (in Lucian).
185 *turn* deflect (a technical hunting term)
186 *ape's tricks* fantastic or extravagant bowing
191–2 *shifter ... upon't* Trapdoor, posing as a trusty servant, must also be implying
   duplicity: a shifter was a cozener, who would here cunningly remove the 'good
   bit' (or morsel) from under his master's nose. A trencherman or trencher-friend
   was a parasite or toady, and there is probably a hint of this too.
195 *'has* i.e. he has
199–200 The same quip appears in *Michaelmas Term*, III.i.146.

SIR ALEXANDER
> Didst never, as thou has walked about this town,
> Hear of a wench called Moll, mad merry Moll?

TRAPDOOR
> Moll Cutpurse, sir?

SIR ALEXANDER   The same, dost thou know her then?

TRAPDOOR
> As well as I know 'twill rain upon Simon and Jude's day
> next: I will sift all the taverns i'th'city, and drink half-pots   205
> with all the watermen o'th'Bankside, but if you will, sir, I'll
> find her out.

SIR ALEXANDER
> That task is easy, do't then. Hold thy hand up:
> What's this? Is't burnt?

TRAPDOOR
> No sir, no, a little singed with making fireworks.   210

SIR ALEXANDER
> There's money, spend it: that being spent, fetch more.

TRAPDOOR
> Oh sir, that all the poor soldiers in England had such a
> leader! For fetching, no water-spaniel is like me.

SIR ALEXANDER
> This wench we speak of strays so from her kind
> Nature repents she made her. 'Tis a mermaid   215
> Has tolled my son to shipwreck.

TRAPDOOR
> I'll cut her comb for you.

SIR ALEXANDER
> I'll tell out gold for thee then: hunt her forth,
> Cast out a line hung full of silver hooks
> To catch her to thy company: deep spendings   220
> May draw her that's most chaste to a man's bosom.

204 *Simon and Jude's day* 28 October, the day on which the pageants put on by the
   City Livery companies turned out, was proverbially stormy: 'Simon and Jude all
   the ships on the sea home do they crowd' (see V. S. Lean, *Collectanea* (1902–4),
   I, 381).
206 *watermen o'th'Bankside* 'Taylor the water-poet asserts that at this time, between
   Windsor and Gravesend, there were not fewer than forty thousand watermen'
   (Reed, qu. Collier).
209 *burnt* i.e. branded (as a convicted criminal's would be)
215 *a mermaid* Mermaids were generally regarded as sinister and often identified
   with the Sirens (female monsters with ravishing voices whose singing lured
   sailors to shipwreck).
217 *I'll cut her comb* An ancient proverbial phrase: cutting a cock's comb was a usual
   accompaniment of gelding. So Trapdoor will destroy Moll's masculinity. The
   phrase also suggests clitorectomy.

TRAPDOOR
The jingling of golden bells, and a good fool with a hobby-
horse, will draw all the whores i'th'town to dance in a
morris.
SIR ALEXANDER
Or rather (for that's best – they say sometimes   225
She goes in breeches) follow her as her man.
TRAPDOOR
And when her breeches are off, she shall follow me.
SIR ALEXANDER
Beat all thy brains to serve her.
TRAPDOOR
Zounds sir, as country wenches beat cream, till butter
comes.   230
SIR ALEXANDER
Play thou the subtle spider, weave fine nets
To ensnare her very life.
TRAPDOOR   Her life?
SIR ALEXANDER   Yes, suck
Her heart-blood if thou canst: twist thou but cords
To catch her, I'll find law to hang her up.
TRAPDOOR
Spoke like a worshipful bencher.   235
SIR ALEXANDER
Trace all her steps: at this she-fox's den
Watch what lambs enter: let me play the shepherd
To save their throats from bleeding, and cut hers.
TRAPDOOR
This is the goll shall do't.
SIR ALEXANDER   Be firm, and gain me
Ever thine own. This done, I entertain thee: 240
How is thy name?
TRAPDOOR
My name, sir, is Ralph Trapdoor, honest Ralph.

222–3 *hobby-horse* The still common children's toy was already well known and frequently appears as part of the fool's equipment. But a hobby-horse was also a
pantomime horse which had an important place in the morris dance: it was
formed by a man inside a frame with the head and tail of a horse (*Sh. Eng.*, II,
438). 'Morris', however, was also used loosely of any rather wild dance, and
'hobby-horse' commonly of a wanton.
228 *serve* not just as a servant but as a stallion serves a mare
235 *bencher* magistrate
239 *goll* cant term for hand
240 *entertain thee* take thee into my service
242 *Ralph* (pronounced – and sometimes spelt – Rafe) a common name for servants
in contemporary plays: cf. *A Mad World, My Masters*, III.i.5.

SIR ALEXANDER
Trapdoor, be like thy name, a dangerous step
For her to venture on, but unto me –
TRAPDOOR
As fast as your sole to your boot or shoe, sir.   245
SIR ALEXANDER
Hence then, be little seen here as thou canst,
I'll still be at thine elbow.
TRAPDOOR   The trapdoor's set.
Moll, if you budge y'are gone, this me shall crown:
A roaring boy the roaring girl puts down.
SIR ALEXANDER
God-'a'-mercy, lose no time.   *Exeunt* 250

[Act II, Scene i]

The three shops open in a rank: the first a pothecary's shop,
the next a feather-shop, the third a sempster's shop:
MISTRESS GALLIPOT *in the first,* MISTRESS TILTYARD *in*
the next, MASTER OPENWORK *and his* WIFE *in the third.*
To them enters LAXTON, GOSHAWK, *and* GREENWIT

MISTRESS OPENWORK
Gentlemen, what is't you lack? What is't you buy? See fine
bands and ruffs, fine lawns, fine cambrics. What is't you
lack, gentlemen, what is't you buy?
LAXTON
Yonder's the shop.
GOSHAWK
Is that she?   5
LAXTON
Peace.
GREENWIT
She that minces tobacco?
LAXTON
Ay: she's a gentlewoman born, I can tell you, though it be
her hard fortune now to shred Indian pot-herbs.

---

0 sd *in a rank* in a row, side by side
1 *what is't you lack?* The standard street-cry of pedlars, shopmen, apprentices, etc.,
     calling for custom.
7 *minces* shreds; tobacco was commonly sold by apothecaries
9 *Indian pot-herbs* Pot-herbs are simply herbs boiled in a pot; perhaps a misunder-
     standing of how tobacco is prepared.

GOSHAWK

    Oh sir, 'tis many a good woman's fortune, when her hus-   10
band turns bankrupt, to begin with pipes and set up again.

LAXTON

    And indeed the raising of the woman is the lifting up of the
man's head at all times: if one flourish, t'other will bud as
fast, I warrant ye.

GOSHAWK

    Come, th'art familiarly acquainted there, I grope that.   15

LAXTON

    And you grope no better i'th'dark, you may chance lie
i'th'ditch when y'are drunk.

GOSHAWK

    Go, th'art a mystical lecher.

LAXTON

    I will not deny but my credit may take up an ounce of pure
smoke.   20

GOSHAWK

    May take up an ell of pure smock. Away, go. [*Aside*] 'Tis
the closest striker. Life, I think he commits venery forty
foot deep, no man's aware on't. I, like a palpable smockster, go to work so openly with the tricks of art, that I'm as
apparently seen as a naked boy in a vial, and were it not for   25
a gift of treachery that I have in me to betray my friend
when he puts most trust in me – mass, yonder he is, too –
and by his injury to make good my access to her, I should

---

11 *pipes* Tobacco was good business (cf. III.iii.67n.); but 'pipe' is plainly used here
as a cant word for penis (cf. below, 44), as at *Romeo and Juliet*, IV.v.96.

15 *grope* seize, apprehend; there is a common sexual use of the word which here
picks up Laxton's *double entendre*.

18 *mystical* secret (cf. 'Epistle to the Comic Play-Readers', l.23)

21 *take up an ell of pure smock* i.e. lift up a woman's under-skirt (cf. *The Taming of
the Shrew*, IV.iii.158)

22 *closest striker* most secret fornicator

23–4 *smockster* bawd: cf. *Your Five Gallants*, V.ii.45: 'you're a hired smockster ...
we are certified that you're a bawd'

25 *naked boy in a vial* (i.e. phial). Steevens's suggestion – 'I suppose he means an
abortion preserved in spirits' – seems irrelevant and incredible; the point is presumably the visibility of nakedness seen through clear glass. Naked boys is a
popular name for the meadow saffron which flowers after its leaves have with-
ered; but the phrase also occurs in *The Alchemist* (III.iv.80–1) in such a way as
to suggest catamite: 'competent means to keep himself, / His punk, and naked
boy, in excellent fashion'.

appear as defective in courting as a farmer's son the first
day of his feather, that doth nothing at court but woo the   30
hangings and glass windows for a month together, and
some broken waiting-woman for ever after. I find those
imperfections in my venery that, were't not for flattery and
falsehood, I should want discourse and impudence, and he
that wants impudence among women is worthy to be   35
kicked out at bed's feet. He shall not see me yet.

GREENWIT
Troth this is finely shred.

LAXTON
Oh, women are the best mincers.

MISTRESS GALLIPOT
'T had been a good phrase for a cook's wife, sir.

LAXTON
But 'twill serve generally, like the front of a new almanac,   40
as thus: calculated for the meridian of cook's wives, but
generally for all Englishwomen.

MISTRESS GALLIPOT
Nay, you shall ha't, sir, I have filled it for you.

She puts it to the fire

LAXTON
The pipe's in a good hand, and I wish mine always so.

GREENWIT
But not to be used o'that fashion.   45

LAXTON
Oh pardon me, sir, I understand no French. I pray be
covered. Jack, a pipe of rich smoke.

GOSHAWK
Rich smoke? That's sixpence a pipe, is't?

GREENWIT
To me, sweet lady.

MISTRESS GALLIPOT
[*Aside to* LAXTON] Be not forgetful; respect my credit, seem   50

29–30 *the first day of his feather* The feather has been acquired to gentrify his appearance.
32 *broken* violated, also used of unmarried mothers
40 *the front of a new almanac* The predictions in almanacs were calculated for a given
meridian, but could be adapted to cover the whole country.
46 *I understand no French* i.e. he declines the innuendo; cf. V.i.169.
46–7 *be covered* replace your hat (to Goshawk)

strange: art and wit makes a fool of suspicion: pray be
wary.

LAXTON

Push, I warrant you: – come, how is't, gallants?

GREENWIT

Pure and excellent.

LAXTON

I thought 'twas good, you were grown so silent; you are   55
like those that love not to talk at victuals, though they
make a worse noise i'the nose than a common fiddler's
prentice, and discourse a whole supper with snuffling. – I
must speak a word with you anon.

MISTRESS GALLIPOT

Make your way wisely then.   60

GOSHAWK

Oh what else, sir? He's perfection itself, full of manners,
but not an acre of ground belonging to 'em.

GREENWIT

Ay and full of form, h'as ne'er a good stool in's chamber.

GOSHAWK

But above all religious: he preyeth daily upon elder brothers.   65

GREENWIT

And valiant above measure: h'as run three streets from a
sergeant.

LAXTON

Puh, puh.

He blows tobacco in their faces

GREENWIT [*and*] GOSHAWK

Oh, puh, ho, ho.

LAXTON

So, so.   70

MISTRESS GALLIPOT

What's the matter now, sir?

LAXTON

I protest I'm in extreme want of money: if you can supply
me now with any means, you do me the greatest pleasure,

---

51 *art and wit makes a fool of suspicion* This sounds proverbial, but appears not to be
    otherwise recorded. There is a fairly close parallel in *A Mad World, My Masters*
    (I.ii.93–5): 'The way to daunt is to outvie suspect. / Manage these principles but
    with art and life, / Welcome all nations, thou'rt an honest wife.'

61 *manners* with a play on 'manors'

63 *full of form* replete with propriety, with a play on 'form' in the sense of bench

next to the bounty of your love, as ever poor gentleman
tasted.   75

MISTRESS GALLIPOT

What's the sum would pleasure ye, sir? Though you deserve nothing less at my hands.

LAXTON

Why, 'tis but for want of opportunity thou know'st. [*Aside*]
I put her off with opportunity still: by this light I hate her,
but for means to keep me in fashion with gallants: for what   80
I take from her, I spend upon other wenches, bear her in
hand still; she has wit enough to rob her husband, and I
ways enough to consume the money. – Why, how now?
What? The chincough?

GOSHAWK

Thou hast the cowardliest trick to come before a man's   85
face and strangle him ere he be aware: I could find in my
heart to make a quarrel in earnest.

LAXTON

Pox, and thou dost – thou know'st I never use to fight with
my friends – thou'll but lose thy labour in't. – Jack Dapper!

Enter J[ACK] DAPPER, *and his man* GULL

GREENWIT

Monsieur Dapper, I dive down to your ankles.   90

JACK DAPPER

Save ye gentlemen, all three in a peculiar salute.

GOSHAWK

He were ill to make a lawyer, he dispatches three at once.

LAXTON

So, well said. – But is this of the same tobacco, Mistress
Gallipot?

[She gives him money secretly]

MISTRESS GALLIPOT

The same you had at first, sir.   95

---

76 *pleasure* The verb doubtless has here (as currently) the secondary sense of stimu-
   late sexually.
77 *nothing less at my hands* i.e. than her love
81–2 *bear her in hand* deceive her: cf. *Macbeth*, III.i.80; *Cymbeline*, V.v.43
84 *chincough* whooping-cough. Laxton's smoke has made Goshawk cough.
93 *is this of the same tobacco...?* 'She gives him money, and he pretends that he receives only tobacco' (Collier, qu. Bullen).
95 sp MISTRESS GALLIPOT ed. (M. Gal. Q)

LAXTON

I wish it no better: this will serve to drink at my chamber.

GOSHAWK

Shall we taste a pipe on't?

LAXTON

Not of this by my troth, gentlemen, I have sworn before
you.

GOSHAWK

What, not Jack Dapper?   100

LAXTON

Pardon me, sweet Jack, I'm sorry I made such a rash oath,
but foolish oaths must stand: where art going, Jack?

JACK DAPPER

Faith, to buy one feather.

LAXTON

[*Aside*] One feather? The fool's peculiar still.

JACK DAPPER

Gull.   105

GULL

Master?

JACK DAPPER

Here's three halfpence for your ordinary, boy, meet me an
hour hence in Paul's.

GULL

[*Aside*] How? Three single halfpence? Life, this will scarce
serve a man in sauce, a ha'p'orth of mustard, a ha'p'orth   110
of oil and a ha'p'orth of vinegar, what's left then for the
pickle herring? This shows like small beer i'th'morning
after a great surfeit of wine o'er night: he could spend his
three pound last night in a supper amongst girls and brave
bawdy-house boys: I thought his pockets cackled not for   115
nothing, these are the eggs of three pound, I'll go sup 'em
up presently.   *Exit*

LAXTON

[*Aside*] Eight, nine, ten angels: good wench i'faith, and one
that loves darkness well, she puts out a candle with the

---

96 *drink* smoke (a common expression)

107 *three halfpence for your ordinary* An ordinary was a public eating-house that provided fixed-price meals. Bullen quotes from *Father Hubburd's Tales*: 'we ... took
our repast at thrifty Mother Walker's, where we found a whole nest of pinching
bachelors, crowded together upon forms and benches in that most worshipful
three halfpenny ordinary'.

108 *Paul's* i.e. St Paul's, in the nave of which masterless men set up their bills for service. (See *Sh. Eng.*, II, 166.)

115 *cackled* gave away secrets

best tricks of any drugster's wife in England: but that   120
which mads her, I rail upon opportunity still, and take no
notice on't. The other night she would needs lead me into
a room with a candle in her hand to show me a naked picture, where no sooner entered but the candle was sent of
an errand: now I not intending to understand her, but like   125
a puny at the inns of venery, called for another light inno-
cently: thus reward I all her cunning with simple mistak-
ing. I know she cozens her husband to keep me, and I'll
keep her honest as long as I can, to make the poor man
some part of amends: an honest mind of a whoremaster! –   130
How think you amongst you? What, a fresh pipe? Draw in
a third, man.

GOSHAWK
No, you're a hoarder, you engross by th'ounces.

At the feather-shop now

JACK DAPPER
Puh, I like it not.

MISTRESS TILTYARD What feather is't you'd have, sir?
These are most worn and most in fashion   135
Amongst the beaver gallants, the stone riders,
The private stage's audience, the twelvepenny-stool
    gentlemen:
I can inform you 'tis the general feather.

JACK DAPPER
And therefore I mislike it – tell me of general!
Now a continual Simon and Jude's rain   140

---

123 *naked picture* pornographic image
125 *errand* ed. (arrant Q)
126 *puny* freshman
130 *whoremaster* womaniser, lecher
133 *engross* buy up wholesale, especially for reselling at an inflated price
    by th' ed. (bith Q)
134 sp MISTRESS ed. (M. Q): Master Tiltyard is not present
136 *beaver gallants* those wearing beaver hats. Stubbes in the *Anatomy of Abuses* refers
    to beaver hats at 20, 30, and 40 shillings.
    stone riders riders of stallions or, possibly, male homosexuals
137 *The private stage's audience* 'Private' playhouses were devised to circumvent the
    regulations of the Act of Common Council which forbade houses of public
    entertainment within the liberties of the City. The performances, given by chil-
    dren (who were technically in training), were to quite small and select audiences,
    who paid high prices for admission.
    twelvepenny-stool The normal price for the use of a stool was sixpence.
140 *Simon and Jude's rain* cf. I.ii.204 and n.

Beat all your feathers as flat down as pancakes.
Show me – a – spangled feather.
MISTRESS TILTYARD   Oh, to go
A-feasting with? You'd have it for a hench-boy?
You shall.

At the sempster's shop now

MASTER OPENWORK
Mass, I had quite forgot.   145
His honour's footman was here last night, wife,
Ha' you done with my lord's shirt?
MISTRESS OPENWORK   What's that to you, sir?
I was this morning at his honour's lodging,
Ere such a snail as you crept out of your shell.
MASTER OPENWORK
Oh, 'twas well done, good wife.
MISTRESS OPENWORK   I hold it better, sir,   150
Than if you had done't yourself.
MASTER OPENWORK   Nay, so say I:
But is the countess's smock almost done, mouse?
MISTRESS OPENWORK
Here lies the cambric, sir, but wants, I fear me.
MASTER OPENWORK
I'll resolve you of that presently.
MISTRESS OPENWORK
Hey-day! Oh audacious groom,   155
Dare you presume to noblewomen's linen?
Keep you your yard to measure shepherd's holland,
I must confine you, I see that.

At the tobacco shop now

GOSHAWK
What say you to this gear?
LAXTON
I dare the arrant'st critic in tobacco   160

---

141 *as flat down as pancakes* proverbial from an early period
144 *hench-boy?* page; punctuation ed. (hinch-boy, Q)
149 *snail* ed. (snake Q)
153 *wants* i.e. wants finishing, or perhaps there isn't enough material
155 *Hey-day!* ed. (Haida Q)
157 *yard* with a play on 'penis'
    shepherd's holland linen for shepherd's smocks
159 *gear* stuff; but the (then standard English) sense of genitals may be present
160 *arrant'st* ed. (arrants Q) strictest

To lay one fault upon't.

Enter MOLL *in a frieze jerkin and a black saveguard*

GOSHAWK   Life, yonder's Moll.

LAXTON
Moll, which Moll?

GOSHAWK
Honest Moll.

LAXTON
Prithee let's call her. – Moll.

ALL [GALLANTS]
Moll, Moll, pist, Moll.   165

MOLL
How now, what's the matter?

GOSHAWK
A pipe of good tobacco, Moll.

MOLL
I cannot stay.

GOSHAWK
Nay Moll, puh, prithee hark, but one word i'faith.

MOLL
Well, what is't?   170

GREENWIT
Prithee come hither, sirrah.

LAXTON
[*Aside*] Heart, I would give but too much money to be nibbling with that wench: life, sh'as the spirit of four great
parishes, and a voice that will drown all the city: methinks
a brave captain might get all his soldiers upon her, and 175
ne'er be beholding to a company of Mile End milksops, if
he could come on, and come off quick enough: such a
Moll were a marrow-bone before an Italian, he would cry

---

161 sd *frieze jerkin* a jerkin made of coarse woollen cloth
   saveguard an outer petticoat worn by women to protect their dress when riding
175 *get* i.e. beget
176 *Mile End milksops* The city trained-bands were exercised at Mile End on the green which is now Stepney Green; it was also a place of resort for cakes and cream.
178 *marrow-bone before an Italian* Marrow-bone was popularly supposed to be an aphrodisiac. Cf. *A Mad World, My Masters*, I.ii.46ff.: 'I have conveyed away all her wanton pamphlets; as *Hero and Leander, Venus and Adonis*; O, two luscious marrowbone pies for a young married wife!' Italians were widely believed to be extremely lecherous and to be fond of unorthodox coital positions (cf. *Michaelmas Term*, III.i.18, and *A Mad World, My Masters*, III.iii.59). Moll's 'masculinity' might here imply a suggestion of buggery.

bona roba till his ribs were nothing but bone. I'll lay hard
siege to her, money is that aqua fortis that eats into many 180
a maidenhead: where the walls are flesh and blood, I'll
ever pierce through with a golden auger.

GOSHAWK
Now thy judgment, Moll, is't not good?

MOLL
Yes faith 'tis very good tobacco, how do you sell an ounce?
Farewell. God b'i'you, Mistress Gallipot. 185

GOSHAWK
Why Moll, Moll.

MOLL
I cannot stay now i'faith, I am going to buy a shag ruff, the
shop will be shut in presently.

GOSHAWK
'Tis the maddest fantasticall'st girl: — I never knew so
much flesh and so much nimbleness put together. 190

LAXTON
She slips from one company to another like a fat eel between a Dutchman's fingers. — [Aside] I'll watch my time
for her.

MISTRESS GALLIPOT
Some will not stick to say she's a man
And some both man and woman. 195

LAXTON
That were excellent, she might first cuckold the husband
and then make him do as much for the wife.

The feather-shop again

MOLL
Save you; how does Mistress Tiltyard?

JACK DAPPER
Moll.

MOLL
Jack Dapper. 200

JACK DAPPER
How dost Moll?

---

179 *bona roba* wench, frequently a prostitute (the term had lately been taken over
   from Italian)
180 *aqua fortis* literally nitric acid, commonly used in dilute form as a solvent
181 *maidenhead ... I'll* punctuation ed. (maidenhead, where ... bloud. I'll ... Q).
187 *shag* cloth having a velvet nap on one side, usually of worsted but sometimes of
   silk
188 *shut in* The counter-flap projecting from the house to form a shop would be raised.

MOLL

I'll tell thee by and by, I go but to th'next shop.

JACK DAPPER

Thou shalt find me here this hour about a feather.

MOLL

Nay and a feather hold you in play a whole hour, a goose
will last you all the days of your life.   205

The sempster shop

Let me see a good shag ruff.

MASTER OPENWORK

Mistress Mary, that shalt thou i'faith, and the best in the
shop.

MISTRESS OPENWORK

How now, greetings, love-terms with a pox between you,
have I found out one of your haunts? I send you for hol-   210
lands, and you're i'th'low countries with a mischief. I'm
served with good ware by th'shift, that makes it lie dead so
long upon my hands, I were as good shut up shop, for
when I open it I take nothing.

MASTER OPENWORK

Nay and you fall a-ringing once, the devil cannot stop you,   215
I'll out of the belfry as fast as I can. – Moll.

MISTRESS OPENWORK

Get you from my shop.

MOLL

I come to buy.

210–14 *I send you ... nothing* A dazzling linguistic challenge. The first pun seems to
derive in particular from the brilliant wordplay of *2 Henry IV*, II.ii.21–2: 'the rest
of the low countries have made a shift to eat up thy holland': 'low countries'
(with a play on 'cunt' in 'countries' see *Hamlet*, III.ii.116) meant both the lower
parts of the body and the stews (where Poins and supposedly Master Openwork
beget bastards); hence, similarly, 'holland', as well as, literally, linen – which
prompts 'shift' in the sense of chemise. And the seemingly innocent shopkeep-
ing talk in the second sentence conceals a complex obscenity: 'ware' was in regular use for the genitals of either sex, but especially of women (where it was commonly 'lady's ware') (cf. *A Chaste Maid in Cheapside*, II.i.99). The burden, then,
of Mistress Openwork's complaint is that by a trick (a shift) she is left to make
what shift she can by handling her sexual parts (those next to her shift) herself:
a barren ('dead') activity, but she may as well stop offering herself, for when she
opens up her 'shop', nothing comes in.
211 *i'th'low* ed. (ith the low Q)
215 *a-ringing* scolding
216 *Moll* Her name appears at the end of a line seemingly as the last word of
Openwork's speech. But I suspect it may be the speech prefix of a missing few
words from Moll, to which Mistress Openwork's speech is a retort.

MISTRESS OPENWORK
I'll sell ye nothing, I warn ye my house and shop.
MOLL
You goody Openwork, you that prick out a poor living　220
And sews many a bawdy skin-coat together,
Thou private pandress between shirt and smock,
I wish thee for a minute but a man:
Thou should'st never use more shapes; but as th'art
I pity my revenge: now my spleen's up　225
I would not mock it willingly.

Enter a FELLOW *with a long rapier by his side*

　　　　　　　　　　　　　　　　　　　　　– Ha, be thankful,
Now I forgive thee.
MISTRESS OPENWORK　Marry hang thee,
I never asked forgiveness in my life.
MOLL
You, goodman swine's-face.
FELLOW
What, will you murder me?　230
MOLL
You remember, slave, how you abused me t'other night in
a tavern?
FELLOW
Not I, by this light.
MOLL
No, but by candlelight you did, you have tricks to save
your oaths, reservations have you? And I have reserved　235
somewhat for you. [*Strikes him*] As you like that, call for
more, you know the sign again.
FELLOW
Pox on't, had I brought any company along with me to
have borne witness on't, 'twould ne'er have grieved me,
but to be struck and nobody by, 'tis my ill fortune still:　240
why, tread upon a worm, they say 'twill turn tail, but indeed a gentleman should have more manners.　　　*Exit*

219　*warn* deny
220　*goody* shortened form of 'goodwife', a term of civility used to married women of
　　　humble station
221　*skin-coat* a coat made of skins, but used figuratively of a person's skin itself
226　sd FELLOW probably in the sense of thief (cf. *A Trick to Catch the Old One*,
　　　II.i.19f.)
241　*tread . . . tail* i.e. even the humblest will resent extreme ill-treatment: a common
　　　proverbial expression

LAXTON
> Gallantly performed i'faith Moll, and manfully, I love thee
> forever for't: base rogue, had he offered but the least
> counter-buff, by this hand I was prepared for him.   245

MOLL
> You prepared for him? Why should you be prepared for
> him, was he any more than a man?

LAXTON
> No, nor so much by a yard and a handful London
> measure.

MOLL
> Why do you speak this then? Do you think I cannot ride a   250
> stone horse unless one lead him by th'snaffle?

LAXTON
> Yes and sit him bravely, I know thou canst Moll, 'twas but
> an honest mistake through love, and I'll make amends for't
> any way: prithee sweet plump Moll, when shall thou and I
> go out o'town together?   255

MOLL
> Whither? To Tyburn, prithee?

LAXTON
> Mass that's out o'town indeed, thou hang'st so many jests
> upon thy friends still. I mean honestly to Brainford,
> Staines, or Ware.

MOLL
> What to do there?   260

LAXTON
> Nothing but be merry and lie together, I'll hire a coach
> with four horses.

MOLL
> I thought 'twould be a beastly journey: you may leave out
> one well, three horses will serve if I play the jade myself.

248 *London measure* a former practice of London drapers of allowing a little more
   than the standard yard. For the obscene pun on 'yard' cf. II.ii.84n.
250–1 *ride a stone horse* A stone horse is a stallion, likely to be a horse of some spirit;
   but there is likely to be in Laxton's answer a hint of Moll's assumed sexual
   prowess, though 'to ride a horse' was normally used of a man, meaning to mount
   a woman.
256 *Tyburn* a place of execution
258 *Brainford* a common spelling of Brentford, then a popular place for assignations
   (as were Staines and Ware), and one of the most frequently alluded to
263 *beastly* obscene; sexually bestial
264 *play the jade* act the whore: the word was used contemptuously of both horses
   and women

LAXTON

Nay push, th'art such another kicking wench, prithee be   265
kind and let's meet.

MOLL

'Tis hard but we shall meet, sir.

LAXTON

Nay but appoint the place then, there's ten angels in fair
gold, Moll, you see I do not trifle with you, do but say thou
wilt meet me, and I'll have a coach ready for thee.   270

MOLL

Why, here's my hand I'll meet you sir.

LAXTON

[Aside] Oh good gold. – The place, sweet Moll?

MOLL

It shall be your appointment.

LAXTON

Somewhat near Holborn, Moll.

MOLL

In Gray's Inn Fields then.   275

LAXTON

A match.

MOLL

I'll meet you there.

LAXTON

The hour?

MOLL

Three.

LAXTON

That will be time enough to sup at Brainford.   280

Fall from them to the other

MASTER OPENWORK

I am of such a nature, sir, I cannot endure the house when
she scolds, sh'has a tongue will be heard further in a still
morning than Saint Antling's bell, she rails upon me for

---

275 *Gray's Inn Fields* open fields to the north of Gray's Inn, used as an archery
ground, but afterwards frequented by footpads

280 sd *Fall from them to the other* i.e. the other group on the stage come forward or
take over the dialogue

282 *heard* ed. (hard Q)

283 *Saint Antling's bell* St Antholin's Church, which stood in Watling Street, near St
Paul's, was much frequented by Puritans. In 1599 a number of clergymen of
Puritan views established a morning lecture here, the bell for which began to ring
at 5 a.m. and was a great nuisance to the neighbourhood (Sugden). The church,
rebuilt after the Great Fire of 1666, was pulled down in 1874.

foreign wenching, that I being a freeman must needs keep
a whore i'th'suburbs, and seek to impoverish the liberties: 285
when we fall out, I trouble you still to make all whole with
my wife.

GOSHAWK

No trouble at all, 'tis a pleasure to me to join things
together.

MASTER OPENWORK

[*Aside*] Go thy ways, I do this but to try thy honesty,   290
Goshawk.

The feather-shop

JACK DAPPER

How lik'st thou this, Moll?

MOLL

Oh singularly, you're fitted now for a bunch. [*Aside*] He
looks for all the world with those spangled feathers like a
nobleman's bedpost. The purity of your wench would I   295
fain try, she seems, like Kent, unconquered, and I believe
as many wiles are in her – oh, the gallants of these times
are shallow lechers, they put not their courtship home
enough to a wench, 'tis impossible to know what woman
is thoroughly honest, because she's ne'er thoroughly tried: 300
I am of that certain belief there are more queans in this
town of their own making than of any man's provoking;

---

285 *suburbs* those, that is, beyond the liberties of the City which extended the City's
control beyond its bounds. 'Liberties' meant also rights or privileges, and Master
Openwork must be hinting at those of his wife.
294–5 *a nobleman's bedpost* The beds of the wealthy were festooned with rich hangings.
295–6 *The purity of your wench would I fain try* i.e. of Mistress Tiltyard. 'Try' is used
frequently by Middleton in a sexual sense. So De Flores misinterprets Beatrice
in *The Changeling* (II.ii.97ff.). Moll's intention is not acted upon; since the
Tiltyards play so small a part, it may be that an episode has been cancelled.
296 *like Kent, unconquered* It was a boast of Kentishmen that Kent had never been
conquered. At Swanscombe (near Northfleet) in 1066, when William I marched
round the country to secure the coast and the Channel ports, he is traditionally
said to have met the men of Kent and confirmed their possession of all their laws
and privileges. The phrase seems likely to be a direct theft from Drayton, *The
Barons' Wars*, I, 323–4:
  Then those of Kent, unconquered of the rest,
  That to this day maintain their ancient right.
There is also an apposite play on Kent/cunt.
301 *queans* whores

where lies the slackness then? Many a poor soul would
down, and there's nobody will push 'em:
Women are courted but ne'er soundly tried,   305
As many walk in spurs that never ride.

The sempster's shop

MISTRESS OPENWORK
Oh abominable.
GOSHAWK
Nay more, I tell you in private, he keeps a whore i'th'sub-
urbs.
MISTRESS OPENWORK
Oh spital dealing, I came to him a gentlewoman born. I'll   310
show you mine arms when you please, sir.
GOSHAWK
[*Aside*] I had rather see your legs, and begin that way.
MISTRESS OPENWORK
'Tis well known he took me from a lady's service, where I
was well beloved of the steward, I had my Latin tongue,
and a spice of the French before I came to him, and now   315
doth he keep a suburbian whore under my nostrils.
GOSHAWK
There's ways enough to cry quit with him: hark in thine
ear.
MISTRESS OPENWORK
There's a friend worth a million.
MOLL
[*Aside*] I'll try one spear against your chastity, Mistress 320
Tiltyard, though it prove too short by the burr.

Enter RALPH TRAPDOOR

TRAPDOOR
[*Aside*] Mass, here she is. I'm bound already to serve her,
though it be but a sluttish trick. – Bless my hopeful young

---

310 *spital dealing* Spitals were originally lazar houses, but came to be used for
    maimed whores.
314 *my Latin tongue* These phrases might suggest that Mistress Openwork had her-
    self been loose before marriage, especially if 'French' is taken to hint at syphilis.
    'Latin tongue' may be another gesture towards Italian sexual habits.
316 *suburbian* obsolete spelling, commonly used where the reference was to licen-
    tious life there
317 *quit* ed. (quite Q: an obsolete form)
321 *burr* (burgh Q) a broad iron ring on a tilting lance, just behind the place for the
    hand

mistress with long life and great limbs, send her the upper
hand of all bailiffs and their hungry adherents.   325

MOLL
How now, what art thou?

TRAPDOOR
A poor ebbing gentleman, that would gladly wait for the
young flood of your service.

MOLL
My service! What should move you to offer your service to
me, sir?   330

TRAPDOOR
The love I bear to your heroic spirit and masculine womanhood.

MOLL
So sir, put case we should retain you to us, what parts are
there in you for a gentlewoman's service?

TRAPDOOR
Of two kinds, right worshipful: movable and immovable: 335
movable to run of errands, and immovable to stand when
you have occasion to use me.

MOLL
What strength have you?

TRAPDOOR
Strength, Mistress Moll? I have gone up into a steeple, and
stayed the great bell as't has been ringing; stopped a wind-   340
mill going.

MOLL
And never struck down yourself?

TRAPDOOR
Stood as upright as I do at this present.

MOLL trips up his heels, he falls

MOLL
Come, I pardon you for this, it shall be no disgrace to you:

---

328 *young flood* the flow of tide up-river
334 *service* The word, as Christopher Ricks points out (*E in C*, 10 (1960), 296),
     means copulation as well as the duty of a servant. Together with 'stand' (cf.
     I.ii.56–7n.) it makes Trapdoor's farmyard intentions plain. 'Use' also has com-
     monly a sexual meaning of course: so, he will have an erection when she needs
     it.
343 sd here ed. (*at l. 332* Q)

I have struck up the heels of the high German's size ere   345
now. What, not stand?

TRAPDOOR
I am of that nature, where I love I'll be at my mistress' foot
to do her service.

MOLL
Why well said, but say your mistress should receive injury,
have you the spirit of fighting in you, durst you second   350
her?

TRAPDOOR
Life, I have kept a bridge myself, and drove seven at a time
before me.

MOLL
Ay?

TRAPDOOR
(*Aside*) But they were all Lincolnshire bullocks by my   355
troth.

MOLL
Well, meet me in Gray's Inn Fields, between three and
four this afternoon, and upon better consideration we'll retain you.

TRAPDOOR
I humbly thank your good mistress-ship.   360
[*Aside*] I'll crack your neck for this kindness.   *Exit*

MOLL *meets* LAXTON

LAXTON
Remember three.

MOLL
Nay if I fail you, hang me.

LAXTON
Good wench i'faith.

then OPENWORK

MOLL
Who's this?   365

MASTER OPENWORK
'Tis I, Moll.

---

345 *the high German* There are a number of allusions to the high German, who was
evidently a fencer of great size who seems to have spent some considerable time
in London. In *The Owl's Almanac*, 7, Dekker says that he 'cudgelled most of our
English fencers now about a month past'; in Shirley's *The Opportunity* he has
'beaten all the fencers in Europe'; but he was at one time, it seems, imprisoned,
for 'those escape very hardly, like the German out of Wood-street' (*The Curtain
Drawer of the World* (1612, qu. Collier), 27).

MOLL

Prithee tend thy shop and prevent bastards.

MASTER OPENWORK

We'll have a pint of the same wine i'faith, Moll.

[Exeunt MOLL *and* MASTER OPENWORK]

The bell rings

GOSHAWK

Hark the bell rings, come gentlemen.

Jack Dapper, where shall's all munch?   370

JACK DAPPER

I am for Parker's ordinary.

LAXTON

He's a good guest to'm, he deserves his board,

He draws all the gentlemen in a term-time thither:

We'll be your followers, Jack, lead the way:

Look you by my faith the fool has feathered his nest well.   375

Exeunt GALLANTS

Enter MASTER GALLIPOT, MASTER TILTYARD, *and*
SERVANTS *with water-spaniels and a duck*

MASTER TILTYARD

Come shut up your shops: where's Master Openwork?

MISTRESS GALLIPOT

Nay ask not me, Master Tiltyard.

MASTER TILTYARD

Where's his water-dog? Puh – pist – hur – hur – pist.

MASTER GALLIPOT

Come wenches come, we're going all to Hogsden.

MISTRESS GALLIPOT

To Hogsden, husband?   380

368 *a pint of the same wine* Bastard was a sweet Spanish wine resembling Muscadel.
     sd 2 *The bell rings* i.e. a clock strikes
371 *Parker's* unidentified
372 *to'm* (*stet* Q); meaning 'to him' not 'to them'
375 sd 3 *water-spaniels and a duck* They are going duck-hunting – a sport in which
     ducks were pursued over a pond.
377 sp MISTRESS GALLIPOT Perhaps this speech should be given to Mistress
     Openwork, to whom the question would be more appropriately put, and from
     whom the reply would be more pointed.
378 *Puh – pist* ... cf. l. 383
381 *Hogsden* i.e. Hoxton, then much resorted to for excursions by citizens and ap-
     prentices *pigsney* (i.e. pig's eye) darling, pet

MASTER GALLIPOT
  Ay, to Hogsden, pigsney.
MISTRESS GALLIPOT
  I'm not ready, husband.
MASTER GALLIPOT
  Faith that's well – hum – pist – pist.

                    Spits in the dog's mouth

  Come Mistress Openwork, you are so long.
MISTRESS OPENWORK
  I have no joy of my life, Master Gallipot.   385
MASTER GALLIPOT
  Push, let your boy lead his water-spaniel along, and we'll
  show you the bravest sport at Parlous Pond. Hey Trug,
  hey Trug, hey Trug, here's the best duck in England, ex-
  cept my wife;
  Hey, hey, hey, fetch, fetch, fetch, come let's away.   390
  Of all the year this is the sportfull'st day.   [*Exeunt*]

                    [Act II, Scene ii]

                    Enter SEBASTIAN *solus*

SEBASTIAN
  If a man have a free will, where should the use
  More perfect shine than in his will to love?
  All creatures have their liberty in that,

                    Enter SIR ALEXANDER *and listens to him*

383 sd *Spits in the dog's mouth* Mulholland quotes William Fennor: 'When a poore
    man comes nigh a churlish mastiffe he must not spurne at him if he meane to go
    quietly by him, but flatter and stroake him on the backe, and spit in his mouth'
    (*Compters Commonwealth*, 1617, p. 73).
387 *Parlous Pond* Parlous or Perilous Pool (so called because it was the scene of many
    accidents) was a large pond lying behind St Luke's Hospital on the edge of
    Hoxton; it was a favourite place for duck-hunting and later for bathing. Though
    both 'pond' and 'sport' make sexual openings, it seems to be literal wildfowl that
    the citizens are going after.

  0 sd *solus* (Lat.) alone
  1 *free will* a key but problematic Christian tenet under pressure from Calvinist no-
    tions of predestination. A character called Freevill appears in Marston's *The
    Dutch Courtesan* (1605).
  5 *there* ed. (there, Q)

Though else kept under servile yoke and fear,
The very bondslave has his freedom there.   5
Amongst a world of creatures voiced and silent
Must my desires wear fetters? – Yea, are you
So near? Then I must break with my heart's truth,
Meet grief at a back way. – Well: why, suppose
The two-leaved tongues of slander or of truth   10
Pronounce Moll loathsome: if before my love
She appear fair, what injury have I?
I have the thing I like: in all things else
Mine own eye guides me, and I find 'em prosper:
Life, what should ail it now? I know that man   15
Ne'er truly loves – if he gainsay't he lies –
That winks and marries with his father's eyes.
I'll keep mine own wide open.

Enter MOLL *and a* PORTER *with a viol on his back*

SIR ALEXANDER   Here's brave wilfulness,
A made match, here she comes, they met o'purpose.
PORTER
Must I carry this great fiddle to your chamber, Mistress   20
Mary?
MOLL
Fiddle, goodman hog-rubber? Some of these porters bear
so much for others, they have no time to carry wit for
themselves.

---

6 *silent* ed. (silent. Q)

7 *fetters?* ed. (fetters – Q)

9 *why, suppose* ed. (why suppose. Q)

10 *two-leaved* ed. (two leaud Q) After some hesitation I follow Dyce and later editors. Collier suggested 'lewd', for which 'leaud' is a recorded contemporary
spelling (Holland's *Pliny*, 1601, I, 31), and we should presumably then understand it in the sense of unlearned or ignorant. Bowers explains 'two-leaved' as a
'comparison of the tongue to the two hinged parts of a door or gate [i.e. equivalent to the Latin *valvae*; cf. Isaiah 45, 1], each of which can move independently and thus pronounce either slander or truth', and he gives 'double-
tongued' as a modern equivalent. The aptness of the comparison is
uncompelling, though the singular 'tongue' would improve matters. But this
reading may be preferred.

22 *Fiddle* There is evidently some joke here which I haven't been able to uncover.
By the eighteenth century, 'fiddle' had become one of many words for the female sexual organs, and it could also mean a writ to arrest; but neither seems to
have much appropriateness here. Cf., however, *Henry VIII*, I.iii.39–41: 'The sly
whoresons / Have got a speeding trick to lay down ladies; / A French song and
a fiddle has no fellow.'

hog-rubber used as a term of contempt, probably not clearly distinguished from
'hog-grubber', a mean or sneaking fellow

PORTER

To your own chamber, Mistress Mary?   25

MOLL

Who'll hear an ass speak? Whither else, goodman pageant-
bearer? They're people of the worst memories.

Exit PORTER

SEBASTIAN

Why, 'twere too great a burthen, love, to have them carry
things in their minds and o'their backs together.

MOLL

Pardon me sir, I thought not you so near.   30

SIR ALEXANDER

So, so, so.

SEBASTIAN

I would be nearer to thee, and in that fashion
That makes the best part of all creatures honest.
No otherwise I wish it.

MOLL

Sir, I am so poor to requite you, you must look for nothing   35
but thanks of me: I have no humour to marry, I love to lie
o'both sides o'th'bed myself, and again o'th'other side; a
wife you know ought to be obedient, but I fear me I am too
headstrong to obey, therefore I'll ne'er go about it. I love
you so well, sir, for your good will I'd be loath you should   40
repent your bargain after, and therefore we'll ne'er come
together at first. I have the head now of myself, and am
man enough for a woman; marriage is but a chopping and
changing, where a maiden loses one head and has a worse
i'th'place.   45

SIR ALEXANDER

The most comfortablest answer for a roaring girl
That ever mine ears drunk in.

SEBASTIAN   This were enough
Now to affright a fool forever from thee,
When 'tis the music that I love thee for.

SIR ALEXANDER

There's a boy spoils all again.   50

MOLL

Believe it, sir, I am not of that disdainful temper, but I
could love you faithfully.

26–7 *pageant-bearer* A pageant was a portable stage, consisting of boards resting on
   a framework of trestles, which could be set up in the street for the acting of plays
   or other spectacles. I do not know why pageant-bearers should have been noted
   for forgetfulness.

42 *at first* in the first place

SIR ALEXANDER

A pox on you for that word. I like you not now,
Y'are a cunning roarer. I see that already.

MOLL

But sleep upon this once more, sir, you may chance shift a   55
mind tomorrow: be not too hasty to wrong yourself, never
while you live, sir, take a wife running, many have run out
at heels that have done't: you see, sir, I speak against myself, and if every woman would deal with their suitor so
honestly, poor younger brothers would not be so often   60
gulled with old cozening widows, that turn o'er all their
wealth in trust to some kinsman, and make the poor
gentleman work hard for a pension. Fare you well sir.

SEBASTIAN

Nay prithee one word more.

SIR ALEXANDER

How do I wrong this girl, she puts him off still.   65

MOLL

Think upon this in cold blood, sir, you make as much
haste as if you were going upon a sturgeon voyage, take de-
liberation, sir, never choose a wife as if you were going to
Virginia.

SEBASTIAN

And so we parted, my too cursed fate.   70

SIR ALEXANDER

She is but cunning, gives him longer time in't.

Enter a TAILOR

TAILOR

Mistress Moll, Mistress Moll: so ho ho so ho.

67 *sturgeon voyage OED* can only suggest a voyage for sturgeon, which scarcely explains what Moll means; probably, like the reference to Virginia, the allusion is
to a voyage of long duration for which any wife would be better than none. But
sturgeons were found in the Thames, and the Lord Mayor had the right to all
caught above London Bridge.

68–9 *as if you were going to Virginia* Presumably because there would be no chance
of finding a wife once there, one must take one from home; but there may be an
obscure play on the name of the colony. And cf. Thomas Harvey's exploits mentioned above, p. xiii.

70 Dyce suggests a quotation here, but none has been located.

72 *so ho ho so ho* This is a customary falconer's cry, encouraging the bird to stoop
to the lure. Hence 'hawking' in the next line, and perhaps the 'red clout'. The
lure was a bunch of feathers sewn on to cloth, sometimes with a piece of red
meat in the middle; in the tailor's case the 'clout' seems likely to have been a pin-
cushion worn strapped to the wrist or finger. 'There boy' was a huntsman's cry
to his dogs: cf. *The Tempest*, IV.i.257.

MOLL

There boy, there boy, what, dost thou go a-hawking after
me with a red clout on thy finger?

TAILOR

I forgot to take measure on you for your new breeches.   75

SIR ALEXANDER

Hoyda, breeches? What, will he marry a monster with two
trinkets? What age is this? If the wife go in breeches, the
man must wear long coats like a fool.

MOLL

What fiddling's here? Would not the old pattern have
served your turn?   80

TAILOR

You change the fashion, you say you'll have the great
Dutch slop, Mistress Mary.

MOLL

Why sir, I say so still.

TAILOR

Your breeches then will take up a yard more.

MOLL

Well, pray look it be put in then.   85

TAILOR

It shall stand round and full, I warrant you.

MOLL

Pray make 'em easy enough.

TAILOR

I know my fault now, t'other was somewhat stiff between
the legs, I'll make these open enough, I warrant you.

SIR ALEXANDER

Here's good gear towards, I have brought up my son to   90
marry a Dutch slop and a French doublet, a codpiece-
daughter.

---

74 *clout* strip of cloth used as a pin-cushion
76–7 *two trinkets* No slang or cant use is recorded. 'Trinkets' may mean testicles or
(taking account of 'monster') suggest that he thinks her hermaphrodite with the
organs of both sexes.
78 *coats* i.e. petticoats
79 *fiddling* fidgeting, playing about
81–2 *great Dutch slop* wide baggy breeches, then newly in fashion
84 This and the tailor's next three speeches have an obscene pun on 'yard' (=
penis, as at *Love's Labour's Lost*, V.ii.669). Cf. *The Honest Whore*, part 1,
V.ii.259ff.: 'This was her tailor – you cut out her loose-bodied gown, and put in
a yard more than I allowed her.'
90 *gear* clothing, with a secondary sense of business at hand

TAILOR

  So, I have gone as far as I can go.

MOLL

  Why then, farewell.

TAILOR

  If you go presently to your chamber, Mistress Mary, pray   95
  send me the measure of your thigh by some honest body.

MOLL

  Well, sir, I'll send it by a porter presently.   *Exit*

TAILOR

  So you had need, it is a lusty one, both of them would
  make any porter's back ache in England.   *Exit*

SEBASTIAN

  I have examined the best part of man,   100
  Reason and judgment, and in love they tell me
  They leave me uncontrolled: he that is swayed
  By an unfeeling blood past heat of love,
  His springtime must needs err, his watch ne'er goes right
  That sets his dial by a rusty clock.   105

SIR ALEXANDER

  So, and which is that rusty clock, sir, you?

SEBASTIAN

  The clock at Ludgate, sir, it ne'er goes true.

SIR ALEXANDER

  But thou goest falser: not thy father's cares
  Can keep thee right. When that insensible work
  Obeys the workman's art, lets off the hour   110
  And stops again when time is satisfied:
  But thou run'st on, and judgment, thy main wheel,

---

98 *a lusty one* Thighs are an obvious incitement to sexual adventure. Cf. *Romeo and Juliet* II.i.19f.: Rosaline's 'quivering thigh, / And the demesnes that there adjacent lie'.

102–5 *he that is swayed ... rusty clock* This seems to be a rather laboured attempt to combine a sardonic comment on the old man's incapacity – once he is old and impotent he cannot hope for sexual success, his spring is no longer taut, his action is rusty, his rhythm erratic and weak – with a warning that the young (those in their springtime) be not ruled by the dicta of the elderly.

107 *The clock at Ludgate* perhaps the clock on St Martin's Church. Old engravings show no clock on the gate itself, which (a replacement of the original) was rebuilt in 1586.

109–11 *When that insensible work ... satisfied* When the invisible movement (of the clock) obeys the workman's art, the hour strikes and stops again after the correct number of strokes. (Lets off = removes the stop from the strike.)

Beats by all stops, as if the work would break,
Begun with long pains for a minute's ruin:
Much like a suffering man brought up with care,   115
At last bequeathed to shame and a short prayer.

SEBASTIAN
I taste you bitterer than I can deserve, sir.

SIR ALEXANDER
Who has bewitched thee, son? What devil or drug
Hath wrought upon the weakness of thy blood,
And betrayed all her hopes to ruinous folly?   120
Oh wake from drowsy and enchanted shame,
Wherein thy soul sits with a golden dream
Flattered and poisoned. I am old, my son,
Oh let me prevail quickly,
For I have weightier business of mine own   125
Than to chide thee: I must not to my grave
As a drunkard to his bed, whereon he lies
Only to sleep, and never cares to rise.
Let me dispatch in time, come no more near her.

SEBASTIAN
Not honestly? Not in the way of marriage?   130

SIR ALEXANDER
What sayst thou, marriage? In what place? The sessions
house? And who shall give the bride, prithee? An indict-
ment?

SEBASTIAN
Sir, now ye take part with the world to wrong her.

SIR ALEXANDER
Why, wouldst thou fain marry to be pointed at?   135
Alas the number's great, do not o'erburden't:
Why, as good marry a beacon on a hill,
Which all the country fix their eyes upon,
As her thy folly doats on. If thou long'st
To have the story of thy infamous fortunes   140
Serve for discourse in ordinaries and taverns,
Th'art in the way: or to confound thy name,
Keep on, thou canst not miss it: or to strike
Thy wretched father to untimely coldness,

---

113 *Beats by all stops* See 109–11n.; but a stop is also a device to prevent overwind-
    ing.
116 *short prayer* i.e. before execution: cf. III.i.118–19
118 *bewitched* ed. (bewitch Q)
120 *all her hopes* Blood may be thought of as feminine by analogy with soul; or poss-
    ibly we should read 'my' or 'thy'.
131–2 *sessions house* legislative court

Keep the left hand still, it will bring thee to't.   145
Yet if no tears wrung from thy father's eyes,
Nor sighs that fly in sparkles from his sorrows,
Had power to alter what is wilful in thee,
Methinks her very name should fright thee from her,
And never trouble me.   150

SEBASTIAN
Why is the name of Moll so fatal, sir?

SIR ALEXANDER
Many one, sir, where suspect is entered,
Forseek all London from one end to t'other,
More whores of that name than of any ten other.

SEBASTIAN
What's that to her? Let those blush for themselves.   155
Can any guilt in others condemn her?
I've vowed to love her: let all storms oppose me,
That ever beat against the breast of man,
Nothing but death's black tempest shall divide us.

SIR ALEXANDER
Oh folly that can doat on nought but shame!   160

SEBASTIAN
Put case a wanton itch runs through one name
More than another, is that name the worse,
Where honesty sits possessed in't? It should rather
Appear more excellent, and deserve more praise,
When through foul mists a brightness it can raise.   165
Why, there are of the devil's, honest gentlemen,
And well descended, keep an open house,
And some o'th'good man's that are arrant knaves.
He hates unworthily that by rote contemns,
For the name neither saves, nor yet condemns: 170
And for her honesty, I have made such proof on't,
In several forms, so nearly watched her ways,
I will maintain that strict against an army,
Excepting you my father: here's her worst,
Sh'has a bold spirit that mingles with mankind,   175

---

145 *Keep the left hand still* act perversely, or perhaps in feigned friendship only: the
   date seems too early for an allusion to left-handed or morganatic marriage
152 *Many one* many a one (presumably constables)
153 *Forseek* search thoroughly, ransack
161 *Put case* suppose, perhaps with a pun on 'case' meaning vagina (as in *A Chaste
   Maid in Cheapside*, II.i.199)
166 *of the devil's* among those who appear to be of the devil's party
168 *o'th'good man's* an allusion to the proverb 'God is a good man'. Cf. *Much Ado*,
   III.v.36.

But nothing else comes near it: and oftentimes
Through her apparel somewhat shames her birth,
But she is loose in nothing but in mirth:
Would all Molls were no worse.
SIR ALEXANDER
This way I toil in vain and give but aim   180
To infamy and ruin: he will fall,
My blessing cannot stay him: all my joys
Stand at the brink of a devouring flood
And will be wilfully swallowed: wilfully.
But why so vain let all these tears be lost?   185
I'll pursue her to shame, and so all's crossed.   *Exit*
SEBASTIAN
He is gone with some strange purpose, whose effect
Will hurt me little if he shoot so wide,
To think I love so blindly: I but feed
His heart to this match, to draw on th'other,   190
Wherein my joy sits with a full wish crowned,
Only his mood excepted, which must change
By opposite policies, courses indirect:
Plain dealing in this world takes no effect.
This mad girl I'll acquaint with my intent,   195
Get her assistance, make my fortunes known:
'Twixt lovers' hearts she's a fit instrument,
And has the art to help them to their own:
By her advice, for in that craft she's wise,
My love and I may meet, spite of all spies.   *Exit* 200

[Act III, Scene i]

Enter LAXTON *in Gray's Inn Fields with the* COACHMAN

LAXTON
Coachman.
COACHMAN
Here sir.

180 *give but aim* The man who gave aim stood near the butt and showed how far the
   arrow fell from the mark.
192 *change* ed. (change. Q)

LAXTON

There's a tester more, prithee drive thy coach to the
hither end of Marybone Park, a fit place for Moll to get in.

COACHMAN

Marybone Park, sir.   5

LAXTON

Ay, it's in our way thou know'st.

COACHMAN

It shall be done, sir.

LAXTON

Coachman.

COACHMAN

Anon, sir.

LAXTON

Are we fitted with good frampold jades?   10

COACHMAN

The best in Smithfield, I warrant you, sir.

LAXTON

May we safely take the upper hand of any coached velvet
cap or tufftaffety jacket? For they keep a vild swaggering in
coaches nowadays, the highways are stopped with them.

---

3 *tester* sixpence (from the teston of Henry VIII, originally worth a shilling, and so
   called because it carried an image of the king's head: *teste* is the old spelling of
   French *tête* = head)
4 *Marybone Park* Until 1611 Marylebone Manor was crown property: the gardens
   (ultimately incorporated into Regent's Park) were said in *A Fair Quarrel*
   (IV.iv.217ff.) to be suitable as a burial ground for whores and panders because
   it was near Tyburn. The point of Laxton's quip, however, is enriched by the
   linking of a pun on Marybone (= marrow-bone; cf. II.i.178n.) and 'park' in the
   sense of 'the female body as a domain where the lover may freely roam' (Eric
   Partridge, *Shakespeare's Bawdy* (1956), p. 163; cf. *Venus and Adonis*, 231ff.).
10 *frampold* mettlesome, spirited (phrampell Q)
   jades contemptuous term for horses
11 *Smithfield* The worst jades came from Smithfield Market, east of Holborn. Cf. *2
   Henry IV*, I.ii.53ff., and the proverbial 'Who goes to Westminster for a wife, to
   Paul's for a man, and to Smithfield for a horse, may meet with a whore, a knave,
   and a jade.'
   you ed. (your Q)
12 *coached* couched; embroidered with gold. The spelling plays on the coaches that
   follow.
13 *tufftaffety* a kind of taffeta with pile or nap arranged in tufts
   vild vile
14 *nowadays* since the repeal of sumptuary law in 1603 which allowed the newly-
   wealthy middle classes to dress more finely than before. These people also need
   coaches – hitherto luxury items – creating traffic jams.

COACHMAN

My life for yours, and baffle 'em too sir: – why, they are   15
the same jades, believe it, sir, that have drawn all your
famous whores to Ware.

LAXTON

Nay, then they know their business, they need no more in-
structions.

COACHMAN

They're so used to such journeys, sir, I never use whip to   20
'em; for if they catch but the scent of a wench once, they
run like devils.   *Exit* COACHMAN *with his whip*

LAXTON

Fine Cerberus, that rogue will have the start of a thousand
ones, for whilst others trot afoot, he'll ride prancing to hell
upon a coach-horse.   25

Stay, 'tis now about the hour of her appointment, but
yet I see her not. (*The clock strikes three*) Hark what's this?
One, two, three, three by the clock at Savoy: this is the
hour, and Gray's Inn Fields the place, she swore she'd
meet me: ha, yonder's two Inns o' Court men with one   30
wench, but that's not she, they walk toward Islington out
of my way: I see none yet dressed like her, I must look for
a shag ruff, a frieze jerkin, a short sword, and a saveguard,
or I get none: why, Moll, prithee make haste, or the
coachman will curse us anon.   35

Enter MOLL *like a man*

MOLL

[*Aside*] Oh here's my gentleman: if they would keep their
days as well with their mercers as their hours with their
harlots, no bankrupt would give seven score pound for a
sergeant's place, for would you know a catchpoll rightly

---

15 *baffle* pass contemptuously
23 *Cerberus* watchdog of the underworld
28 *Savoy* The great palace, built originally by Simon de Montfort in 1245 and re-
  constructed as a hospital in 1509, was by 1580 the subject of complaints that it
  was used as a nursery by 'great numbers of idle wicked persons, cutpurses, coz-
  eners and such other thieves': see G. L. Gomme, *London* (1914), p. 225.
31 *Islington* a suburb to the north of London and a popular resort
33 *saveguard* see II.i.161 sd n.
36–8 The construction is somewhat obscure, though the general meaning is clear:
  if men were as prompt in paying their mercers' bills as in keeping assignments
  with harlots, it would be worth no-one's while to buy a sergeant's place at an inflated price, for there would no longer be the bankruptcies to provide him a living.
39 *catchpoll* sheriff's officer, especially a bum-bailiff

derived, the corruption of a citizen is the generation of a   40
sergeant. How his eye hawks for venery! – Come, you are
ready sir?

LAXTON
Ready? For what sir?

MOLL
Do you ask that now, sir? Why was this meeting 'pointed?

LAXTON
I thought you mistook me sir.   45
You seem to be some young barrister:
I have no suit in law – all my land's sold,
I praise heaven for't; 't has rid me of much trouble.

MOLL
Then I must wake you, sir, where stands the coach?

LAXTON
Who's this? Moll, honest Moll?   50

MOLL
So young, and purblind? You're an old wanton in your
eyes, I see that.

LAXTON
Th'art admirably suited for the Three Pigeons at
Brainford, I'll swear I knew thee not.

MOLL
I'll swear you did not: but you shall know me now.   55

LAXTON
No, not here, we shall be spied i'faith, the coach is better,
come.

MOLL
Stay.

LAXTON
What, wilt thou untruss a point, Moll?

She puts off her cloak and draws

MOLL
Yes, here's the point that I untruss, 't has but one tag,   60
'twill serve, though, to tie up a rogue's tongue.

40 *corruption* decomposition, ceasing to exist
47 *all my land's sold* another indication of Laxton's lack
53 *Three Pigeons* a well-known inn at Brentford, at one time kept by the famous
actor John Lowin. It is mentioned in *The Alchemist*, V.iv.89, and in other plays.
56 *No, not here* Laxton mistakes Moll's use of 'know'. Coaches were used then as
the back seats of cars are now.
59 *untruss a point* unfasten a tag of doublet or breeches (as for sexual intercourse:
see *Measure for Measure*, III.ii.179f.)
58 sd *draws* i.e. her sword

LAXTON
How?

MOLL
There's the gold
With which you hired your hackney, here's her pace,
She racks hard, and perhaps your bones will feel it: 65
Ten angels of mine own I've put to thine,
Win 'em and wear 'em.

LAXTON   Hold Moll, Mistress Mary.

MOLL
Draw, or I'll serve an execution on thee
Shall lay thee up till doomsday.

LAXTON
Draw upon a woman? Why, what dost mean, Moll?   70

MOLL
To teach thy base thoughts manners: th'art one of those
That thinks each woman thy fond flexible whore,
If she but cast a liberal eye upon thee;
Turn back her head, she's thine: or, amongst company,
By chance drink first to thee, then she's quite gone,   75
There's no means to help her: nay for a need,
Wilt swear unto thy credulous fellow lechers
That thou art more in favour with a lady
At first sight than her monkey all her lifetime.
How many of our sex, by such as thou   80
Have their good thoughts paid with a blasted name

---

64 *hackney* horse kept for hire, figuratively a prostitute: cf. *The Honest Whore*, part 1, II.i.225f.
   pace her training as a whore (cf. *Pericles*, IV.vi.63)
65 *racks* moves with the gait called a rack 'in which the two feet on each side are lifted almost simultaneously, and the body is left entirely without support between the lifting of one pair and the landing of the other' (*OED*)
67 *Win 'em and wear 'em* a popular proverbial expression, often taking the form 'Win her and wear her' (i.e. as a bride)
68 *Draw ... execution on thee* To serve an execution is to make formal delivery of a process at law. But in addition to her obvious threat of punishing him capitally, Moll's words punningly mock the frustration of Laxton's lecherous intentions; for to 'draw' meant also to expose the penis (as a sword from a scabbard), and an 'execution' a performance of the sexual act (see *Troilus and Cressida*, III.ii.82). Her threat therefore is that she will geld him.
78 *thou art* ed. (th'art Q)
78-9 lineation ed. (That th'art ... first sight / Then her ... Q)
79 *her monkey* Monkeys were popular as pets (and proverbially lascivious); but perhaps the word is here used to mean favourite, though this sense seems not to be otherwise recorded. See, however, the apparently rather nasty quip in *Michaelmas Term*, I.i.299, 'As an old lady delights in a page or monkey'.

That never deserved loosely or did trip
In path of whoredom beyond cup and lip?
But for the stain of conscience and of soul,
Better had women fall into the hands   85
Of an act silent than a bragging nothing,
There's no mercy in't. – What durst move you, sir,
To think me whorish? – A name which I'd tear out
From the high German's throat if it lay ledger there
To dispatch privy slanders against me.   90
In thee I defy all men, their worst hates,
And their best flatteries, all their golden witchcrafts,
With which they entangle the poor spirits of fools.
Distressed needlewomen and trade-fallen wives,
Fish that must needs bite or themselves be bitten,   95
Such hungry things as these may soon be took
With a worm fastened on a golden hook:
Those are the lecher's food, his prey, he watches
For quarrelling wedlocks, and poor shifting sisters,
'Tis the best fish he takes: but why, good fisherman,   100
Am I thought meat for you, that never yet
Had angling rod cast towards me? 'Cause, you'll say,

---

83 *beyond cup and lip* beyond sharing a loving-cup and kissing
85–6 Cf. Shakespeare, Sonnet 121:
> 'Tis better to be vile than vile esteemed,
> When not to be receives reproach of being;
> And the just pleasure lost, which is so deemed
> Not by our feeling, but by others' seeing.

'Act' here refers to the act of procreation (as, e.g., at *Merchant of Venice*, I.iii.83).
89 *high German's throat* Cf. II.i.345n.
    lay ledger rested permanent, as a fixture
93 *entangle the poor spirits of fools* i.e. endanger their souls by tempting them to sin
    fools. ed. (fooles, Q)
94 *wives,* ed. (wiues. Q)
97 To angle with a golden hook is an ancient proverbial expression; cf. *A Fair Quarrel*, III.ii.123: 'Thou'st fished with silver hooks and golden baits.' 'Fish' was common contemptuous slang for women.
99 *wedlocks* Anthony B. Dawson suggests that 'wedlocks' here means 'marriages' and not, as others have glossed, 'wives'. 'Mistress Hic and Haec: Representations of Moll Frith', *SEL*, 33 (1993), 404 n. 24.
    poor shifting sisters perhaps frustrated spinsters, those (not necessarily literal sisters) who are neglected and make what shift they can; but 'shifting' may suggest those who 'shift beds', i.e. are promiscuous: cf. *A Trick to Catch the Old One*, V.ii.167

I'm given to sport, I'm often merry, jest:
Had mirth no kindred in the world but lust?
Oh shame take all her friends then: but howe'er   105
Thou and the baser world censure my life,
I'll send 'em word by thee, and write so much
Upon thy breast, 'cause thou shalt bear't in mind:
Tell them 'twere base to yield, where I have conquered.
I scorn to prostitute myself to a man,   110
I that can prostitute a man to me,
And so I greet thee.

LAXTON   Hear me.
MOLL   Would the spirits
Of all my slanderers were clasped in thine,
That I might vex an army at one time.

LAXTON
I do repent me, hold.   115

They fight

MOLL
You'll die the better Christian then.

LAXTON
I do confess I have wronged thee, Moll.

MOLL
Confession is but poor amends for wrong,
Unless a rope would follow.

LAXTON   I ask thee pardon.

MOLL
I'm your hired whore, sir.   120

LAXTON
I yield both purse and body.

MOLL   Both are mine,
And now at my disposing.

LAXTON   Spare my life.

103–5 Cf. *The Merry Wives of Windsor*, IV.ii.105–6: 'Wives may be merry, and yet
     honest too: / We do not act that often jest and laugh.'
104 *Had* Perhaps we should read 'Hath' (unless the clause is subordinate to what fol-
     lows): 'Had' may have been attracted by the same word two lines above. The
     line might, however, be a hypothetical, subordinate to the following clause.
108 *'cause* so that
109 *them* i.e. lechers' future victims
113 *slanderers* ed. (slanders Q)
118 *Confession* Moll picks up the word in the sense of auricular confession (cf.
     I.i.39n.), which would precede the shriving of a condemned man immediately
     before execution, cf. II.ii.116.

MOLL

    I scorn to strike thee basely.

LAXTON

    Spoke like a noble girl, i'faith. [*Aside*] Heart, I think I fight
    with a familiar, or the ghost of a fencer, sh'has wounded   125
    me gallantly: call you this a lecherous voyage? Here's
    blood would have served me this seven year in broken
    heads and cut fingers, and it now runs all out together. Pox
    o'the Three Pigeons, I would the coach were here now to
    carry me to the chirurgeons.   130

                                                     Exit

MOLL

    If I could meet my enemies one by one thus,
    I might make pretty shift with 'em in time,
    And make 'em know, she that has wit and spirit
    May scorn to live beholding to her body for meat,
    Or for apparel, like your common dame   135
    That makes shame get her clothes to cover shame.
    Base is that mind that kneels unto her body,
    As if a husband stood in awe on's wife;
    My spirit shall be mistress of this house,
    As long as I have time in't. – Oh,   140

                    Enter TRAPDOOR

    Here comes my man that would be: 'tis his hour.
    Faith, a good well-set fellow, if his spirit
    Be answerable to his umbles; he walks stiff,
    But whether he will stand to't stiffly, there's the point;
    Has a good calf for't, and ye shall have many a woman   145
    Choose him she means to make her head by his calf;
    I do not know their tricks in't. Faith, he seems
    A man without; I'll try what he is within.

TRAPDOOR

    She told me Gray's Inn Fields 'twixt three and four,
    I'll fit her mistress-ship with a piece of service,   150

---

125 *familiar* familiar spirit
126 *voyage* ed. (viage Q: *an obsolete form*)
130 *chirurgeons* rhymes loosely with 'Three Pigeons'
135 *common* i.e. to the whole town
143 *answerable to his umbles* in accord with his insides, or rather, here, the figure he
    makes (umbles are the edible inward parts of an animal, especially deer)
146 *make* ed. (meke Q)
147 *their tricks in't* how they do it

I'm hired to rid the town of one mad girl.

She jostles him

What a pox ails you, sir?

MOLL
He begins like a gentleman.

TRAPDOOR
Heart, is the field so narrow, or your eyesight?
Life, he comes back again.   155

She comes towards him

MOLL
Was this spoke to me, sir?

TRAPDOOR
I cannot tell, sir.

MOLL
Go, y'are a coxcomb.

TRAPDOOR
Coxcomb?

MOLL
Y'are a slave.   160

TRAPDOOR
I hope there's law for you, sir.

MOLL
Yea, do you see, sir?

Turn[s] his hat

TRAPDOOR
Heart, this is no good dealing, pray let me know what
house you're of.

MOLL
One of the Temple, sir.   165

Fillips him

TRAPDOOR
Mass, so methinks.

MOLL
And yet sometime I lie about Chick Lane.

---

162 *Yea* ed. (Ye Q)
165 sd *Fillips him* flicks him with her finger
167 *Chick Lane* later called West Street: a particularly infamous lurking-place of
    thieves in the notorious area around Turnmill Street between Clerkenwell Green
    and Smithfield

TRAPDOOR

    I like you the worse because you shift your lodging so often: I'll not meddle with you for that trick, sir.

MOLL

    A good shift, but it shall not serve your turn.   170

TRAPDOOR

    You'll give me leave to pass about my business, sir.

MOLL

    Your business? I'll make you wait on me before I ha' done, and glad to serve me too.

TRAPDOOR

    How sir? Serve you? Not if there were no more men in England.   175

MOLL

    But if there were no more women in England, I hope you'd wait upon your mistress then.

TRAPDOOR

    Mistress!

MOLL

    Oh you're a tried spirit at a push, sir.

TRAPDOOR

    What would your worship have me do?   180

MOLL

    You a fighter?

TRAPDOOR

    No, I praise heaven, I had better grace and more manners.

MOLL

    As how, I pray, sir?

TRAPDOOR

    Life, 't had been a beastly part of me to have drawn my weapons upon my mistress; all the world would'a' cried   185
shame of me for that.

MOLL

    Why, but you knew me not.

TRAPDOOR

    Do not say so, mistress. I knew you by your wide straddle, as well as if I had been in your belly.

MOLL

    Well, we shall try you further, i'th'meantime we give you   190
entertainment.

---

188 *your wide straddle* apparently simply a characteristic of Moll's (a habit of stand-
    ing with her feet wide astride)
189 *in your belly* suggests sexual intercourse, which might demand a wide straddle
190–1 *give you entertainment* take you into our service

TRAPDOOR
Thank your good mistress-ship.
MOLL
How many suits have you?
TRAPDOOR
No more suits than backs, mistress.
MOLL
Well, if you deserve, I cast off this next week,   195
And you may creep into't.
TRAPDOOR   Thank your good worship.
MOLL
Come follow me to St Thomas Apostle's,
I'll put a livery cloak upon your back
The first thing I do.
TRAPDOOR   I follow my dear mistress.   *Exeunt*

[Act III, Scene ii]

Enter MISTRESS GALLIPOT *as from supper, her husband*
after her

MASTER GALLIPOT
What Pru, nay sweet Prudence.
MISTRESS GALLIPOT
What a pruing keep you, I think the baby would have a teat
it kyes so: pray be not so fond of me, leave your city hu-
mours, I'm vexed at you to see how like a calf you come
bleating after me.   5
MASTER GALLIPOT
Nay, honey Pru: how does your rising up before all the
table show? And flinging from my friends so uncivilly? Fie
Prue, fie, come.

---

194 *backs* Bullen prints 'blacks' – presumably a misprint.
195 *this* i.e. this suit that she is wearing
197 *St Thomas Apostle's* The church was east of St Paul's, near College Hill: it was
   not rebuilt after the fire. The street in which it stood was the resort of fishermen
   and famous for fish dinners; clothiers' shops were in the neighbourhood.

  2 *pruing* There is conceivably a play on the dialect word 'proo', which means to
   call an animal to a stand.
  3 *kyes* i.e. cries; (baby-talk)

MISTRESS GALLIPOT

Then up and ride, i'faith.

MASTER GALLIPOT

Up and ride? Nay, my pretty Pru, that's far from my   10
thought, duck: why, mouse, thy mind is nibbling at something, what is't? What lies upon thy stomach?

MISTRESS GALLIPOT

Such an ass as you: hoyda, y'are best turn midwife, or
physician: y'are a pothecary already, but I'm none of your
drugs.   15

MASTER GALLIPOT

Thou art a sweet drug, sweetest Pru, and the more thou
art pounded, the more precious.

MISTRESS GALLIPOT

Must you be prying into a woman's secrets: say ye?

MASTER GALLIPOT

Woman's secrets?

MISTRESS GALLIPOT

What? I cannot have a qualm come upon me but your   20
teeth waters till your nose hang over it.

MASTER GALLIPOT

It is my love, dear wife.

MISTRESS GALLIPOT

Your love? Your love is all words; give me deeds, I cannot
abide a man that's too fond over me, so cookish; thou dost
not know how to handle a woman in her kind.   25

MASTER GALLIPOT

No, Pru? Why, I hope I have handled –

MISTRESS GALLIPOT

Handle a fool's head of your own, – fie – fie.

MASTER GALLIPOT

Ha, ha, 'tis such a wasp; it does me good now to have her
sting me, little rogue.

---

9 *ride* Is Mistress Gallipot picking up a sexual suggestion in her husband's last
word and possibly in 'honey' as well? Certainly it seems there in her next speech.
'Ride' was Standard English for sexual intercourse (cf. below, l. 179).

12 *what is't* ed. (whats ist Q)

15 *drugs* The word was still in use as a form of 'drudges' which it puns on.

21 *teeth waters* a variant form of 'mouth waters'

24 *cookish* like a cook, perhaps a nonce word

25 *in her kind* as she deserves, as is proper

27 *fool's head* head empty of sense, perhaps again with a sexual *double entendre*

29 *sting* ed. (sing Q); arouse sexually (and cf. *The Taming of the Shrew*, II.i.213f.)

MISTRESS GALLIPOT
　　Now fie how you vex me, I cannot abide these apron hus-　30
　　bands: such cotqueans, you overdo your things, they be-
　　come you scurvily.
MASTER GALLIPOT
　　[*Aside*] Upon my life she breeds, heaven knows how I have
　　strained myself to please her, night and day: I wonder why
　　we citizens should get children so fretful and untoward in　35
　　the breeding, their fathers being for the most part as gen-
　　tle as milch kine. – Shall I leave thee, my Pru?
MISTRESS GALLIPOT
　　Fie, fie, fie.
MASTER GALLIPOT
　　Thou shalt not be vexed no more, pretty kind rogue, take
　　no cold, sweet Pru.　　　　　　　　　　　　　　*Exit*　40
MISTRESS GALLIPOT
　　As your wit has done. Now Master Laxton, show your
　　head, what news from you? Would any husband suspect
　　that a woman crying 'Buy any scurvy-grass' should bring
　　love letters amongst her herbs to his wife? Pretty trick, fine
　　conveyance: had jealousy a thousand eyes, a silly woman　45
　　with scurvy-grass blinds them all;
　　Laxton, with bays
　　Crown I thy wit for this, it deserves praise.
　　This makes me affect thee more, this proves thee wise,
　　'Lack, what poor shift is love forced to devise!　　　　　50
　　– To th' point.

She reads the letter

'Oh sweet creature –' (a sweet beginning) 'pardon my long
absence, for thou shalt shortly be possessed with my presence; though Demophon was false to Phyllis, I will be to

30 *apron husbands* (aperne Q) husbands who follow their wives as if tied to their
　　apron strings (Collier)
31 *cotqueans* used contemptuously of men who act the housewife and meddle in the
　　women's province; Bullen's view that the work is a variant form of 'cock-quean'
　　or 'cuckquean' (a female cuckold) seems unacceptable, and, unusually, no sex-
　　ual quibble seems intended
33 *breeds* Gallipot takes his wife's capricious irritability as a sign of pregnancy.
33–7 Gallipot inadvertently hints at the kind of class miscegenation by which the
　　gentry impregnate female citizens.
43 *scurvy-grass coclearia officinalis*, thought to be anti-scorbutic
54 *Demophon* son of Theseus: Phyllis, a princess of Thrace, hanged herself when he
　　failed to keep his promise to return to her; she was turned into an almond tree
　　which bore leaves when Demophon came at last and embraced it

thee as Pan-da-rus was to Cres-sida: though Aeneas made   55
an ass of Dido, I will die to thee ere I do so; oh sweetest
creature, make much of me, for no man beneath the silver
moon shall make more of a woman than I do of thee: furnish me therefore with thirty pounds, you must do it of
necessity for me; I languish till I see some comfort come   60
from thee; protesting not to die in thy debt, but rather to
live so, as hitherto I have and will,
                              Thy true Laxton ever'.
Alas poor gentleman, troth I pity him,
How shall I raise this money? Thirty pound?   65
'Tis thirty sure, a 3 before an 0,
I know his threes too well. My childbed linen?
Shall I pawn that for him? Then if my mark
Be known I am undone; it may be thought
My husband's bankrupt: which way shall I turn?   70
Laxton, what with my own fears, and thy wants,
I'm like a needle 'twixt two adamants.

Enter MASTER GALLIPOT *hastily*

MASTER GALLIPOT
Nay, nay, wife, the women are all up. [*Aside*] Ha, how,
reading o' letters? I smell a goose, a couple of capons, and
a gammon of bacon from her mother out of the country, I   75
hold my life.
– Steal, steal –
MISTRESS GALLIPOT Oh beshrew your heart.
MASTER GALLIPOT   What letter's that?
I'll see't.

She tears the letter

MISTRESS GALLIPOT Oh would thou hadst no eyes to see
The downfall of me and thyself: I'm forever,
Forever I'm undone.
MASTER GALLIPOT   What ails my Pru?   80
What paper's that thou tear'st?

---

55 *Pan-da-rus ... Cres-sida* so in Q, 'to mark the difficulty with which such hard
    names were read by Mistress Gallipot' (Dyce)
56 *die to thee* punning on the sense of 'spend sexually'
66 *a 3 before an 0* Does she construe his 'three-piece suite' (penis and testicles)
    before a vagina?
68 *mark* laundry mark for identification
72 *adamants* loadstones or magnets
75–6 *I hold my life* by my life, I'm sure of it
77 lineation ed. (*prose* Q)

MISTRESS GALLIPOT   Would I could tear
 My very heart in pieces: for my soul
 Lies on the rack of shame, that tortures me
 Beyond a woman's suffering.
MASTER GALLIPOT   What means this?
MISTRESS GALLIPOT
 Had you no other vengeance to throw down,   85
 But even in height of all my joys –
MASTER GALLIPOT   Dear woman –
MISTRESS GALLIPOT
 When the full sea of pleasure and content
 Seemed to flow over me –
MASTER GALLIPOT   As thou desirest
 To keep me out of bedlam, tell what troubles thee,
 Is not thy child at nurse fallen sick, or dead?   90
MISTRESS GALLIPOT
 Oh no.
MASTER GALLIPOT Heavens bless me, are my barns and houses
 Yonder at Hockley Hole consumed with fire?
 I can build more, sweet Pru.
MISTRESS GALLIPOT   'Tis worse, 'tis worse.
MASTER GALLIPOT
 My factor broke? Or is the Jonas sunk?
MISTRESS GALLIPOT
 Would all we had were swallowed in the waves,   95
 Rather than both should be the scorn of slaves.
MASTER GALLIPOT
 I'm at my wits' end.
MISTRESS GALLIPOT   Oh my dear husband,
 Where once I thought myself a fixed star,
 Placed only in the heaven of thine arms,
 I fear now I shall prove a wanderer;   100
 Oh Laxton, Laxton, is it then my fate

89 *bedlam* Bethlehem hospital for the insane
90 *at nurse* lodged away from home with a wet-nurse
93 *Hockley Hole* Hockley-in-the-Hole was later infamous as the resort of thieves and
   highwaymen, but also a place of amusement: it lay at the centre of what is now
   Clerkenwell. So notorious was it that in 1774 it was thought fitting formally to
   remove its name from the map, and it became Ray Street. Until the late eighteenth century Cold Bath Fields were immediately adjacent to the west.
94 *broke* absconded (or possibly bankrupt)
98 *a fixed star* See note to I.ii.134, and cf. Shakespeare, Sonnet 116: 'love ... is an
   ever-fixed mark, ... the star to every wand'ring bark'. 'Wanderer' here only
   loosely suggests the movement of a meteor, and rather refers to Mistress
   Gallipot's simulated fear that she may prove loose.

To be by thee o'erthrown?
MASTER GALLIPOT   Defend me, wisdom,
  From falling into frenzy. On my knees,
  Sweet Pru, speak, what's that Laxton who so heavy
  Lies on thy bosom?
MISTRESS GALLIPOT   I shall sure run mad.   105
MASTER GALLIPOT
  I shall run mad for company then: speak to me,
  I'm Gallipot thy husband, – Pru, – why Pru,
  Art sick in conscience for some villainous deed
  Thou wert about to act? Didst mean to rob me?
  Tush I forgive thee; hast thou on my bed   110
  Thrust my soft pillow under another's head?
  I'll wink at all faults, Pru, 'las, that's no more
  Than what some neighbours near thee have done before:
  Sweet honey Pru, what's that Laxton?
MISTRESS GALLIPOT   Oh.
MASTER GALLIPOT
  Out with him.
MISTRESS GALLIPOT Oh he's born to be my undoer.   115
  This hand which thou call'st thine, to him was given,
  To him was I made sure i'th'sight of heaven.
MASTER GALLIPOT
  I never heard this thunder.
MISTRESS GALLIPOT   Yes, yes, before
  I was to thee contracted, to him I swore:
  Since last I saw him, twelve months three times told   120
  The moon hath drawn through her light silver bow,
  For o'er the seas he went, and it was said
  (But rumour lies) that he in France was dead.
  But he's alive, oh he's alive, he sent
  That letter to me, which in rage I rent,   125
  Swearing with oaths most damnably to have me,
  Or tear me from this bosom: oh heavens save me.
MASTER GALLIPOT
  My heart will break, – shamed and undone forever.

---

117 *made sure* contracted, betrothed: she is inventing a contract *de praesenti*, sworn
    before witnesses and a canonical impediment to any future marriage to another.
    Such a contract may exist between Sebastian and Mary Fitz-Allard; cf. *A Chaste*
    Maid, IV.i.227, and *A Trick to Catch the Old One*, IV.iv.92, in which play there
    is a scene closely similar to this one.
118 *thunder* menace
120–3 Mistress Gallipot sees herself momentarily as the Empress of Babylon, whose
    speech about the Fairy Queen in *The Whore of Babylon* (I.i.46ff.) she half-re-
    members: 'Five summers have scarce drawn their glimmering nights / Through
    the moon's silver bow...'

MISTRESS GALLIPOT
  So black a day, poor wretch, went o'er thee never.
MASTER GALLIPOT
  If thou should'st wrestle with him at the law,   130
  Th'art sure to fall, no odd sleight, no prevention.
  I'll tell him th'art with child.
MISTRESS GALLIPOT   Hm.
MASTER GALLIPOT   Or give out
  One of my men was ta'en abed with thee.
MISTRESS GALLIPOT
  Hm, hm.
MASTER GALLIPOT Before I lose thee, my dear Pru,
  I'll drive it to that push.
MISTRESS GALLIPOT   Worse, and worse still,   135
  You embrace a mischief, to prevent an ill.
MASTER GALLIPOT
  I'll buy thee of him, stop his mouth with gold,
  Think'st thou 'twill do?
MISTRESS GALLIPOT   Oh me, heavens grant it would;
  Yet now my senses are set more in tune,
  He writ, as I remember in his letter,   140
  That he in riding up and down had spent,
  Ere he could find me, thirty pounds. Send that,
  Stand not on thirty with him.
MASTER GALLIPOT   Forty, Pru,
  Say thou the word, 'tis done: we venture lives
  For wealth, but must do more to keep our wives: 145
  Thirty or forty, Pru?
MISTRESS GALLIPOT   Thirty, good sweet;
  Of an ill bargain let's save what we can,
  I'll pay it him with my tears, he was a man
  When first I knew him of a meek spirit,
  All goodness is not yet dried up I hope.   150
MASTER GALLIPOT
  He shall have thirty pound, let that stop all:
  Love's sweets taste best, when we have drunk down gall.

Enter MASTER TILTYARD *and his wife,* MASTER GOSHAWK,
and MISTRESS OPENWORK

  God-so, our friends; come, come, smooth your cheek;
  After a storm the face of heaven looks sleek.

---

131 *no odd sleight* (slight Q – *a frequent spelling*) no cunning device to prevent her
    being overcome
153 *God-so* a variant form of 'catso', an exclamation of surprise or alarm

MASTER TILTYARD
Did I not tell you these turtles were together?   155
MISTRESS TILTYARD
How dost thou, sirrah? Why, sister Gallipot!
MISTRESS OPENWORK
Lord, how she's changed!
GOSHAWK
Is your wife ill, sir?
MASTER GALLIPOT
Yes indeed, la sir, very ill, very ill, never worse.
MISTRESS TILTYARD
How her head burns, feel how her pulses work.   160
MISTRESS OPENWORK
Sister, lie down a little, that always does me good.
MISTRESS TILTYARD
In good sadness, I find best ease in that too;
Has she laid some hot thing to her stomach?
MISTRESS GALLIPOT
No, but I will lay something anon.
MASTER TILTYARD
Come, come fools, you trouble her, shall's go, Master   165
Goshawk?
GOSHAWK
Yes, sweet Master Tiltyard. – Sirrah Rosamond, I hold my
life Gallipot hath vexed his wife.
MISTRESS OPENWORK
She has a horrible high colour indeed.
GOSHAWK
We shall have your face painted with the same red soon at   170
night, when your husband comes from his rubbers in a
false alley; thou wilt not believe me that his bowls run with
a wrong bias.

---

156 *sirrah* frequently feminine   162 *sadness* seriousness
171–2 *his rubbers in a false alley* Bowls was an exceedingly popular game at this
    period: the alleys were often the scene of gambling and dissipation which nu-
    merous acts of Parliament failed to curb. Cf. Stephen Gosson, *School of Abuse*
    (1579): 'common bowling alleys are privy moths, that eat up the credit of many
    idle citizens, whose gains at home are not able to weigh down their losses
    abroad, whose shops are so far from maintaining their play, that wives and chil-
    dren cry out for bread, and go to bed supperless oft in the year' (*Sh. Eng.*, II,
    465). 'Rubbers' was often a singular form. To bowl out the rubbers 'is to bowl
    a third game for the bets, when the players have gotten one apiece' (Randle
    Holme, *Academy of Armoury*, 1688). Rubbing has also a sexual meaning: cf.
    Love's Labour's Lost, IV.i.138–39, where Costard says 'She's too hard for you at
    pricks sir, challenge her to bowl' and Boyet replies 'I fear too much rubbing.'

MISTRESS OPENWORK
    It cannot sink into me, that he feeds upon stale mutton
    abroad, having better and fresher at home.   175
GOSHAWK
    What if I bring thee where thou shalt see him stand at rack
    and manger?
MISTRESS OPENWORK
    I'll saddle him in's kind, and spur him till he kick again.
GOSHAWK
    Shall thou and I ride our journey then?
MISTRESS OPENWORK
    Here's my hand.   180
GOSHAWK
    No more; come, Master Tiltyard, shall we leap into the
    stirrups with our women, and amble home?
MASTER TILTYARD
    Yes, yes, come wife.
MISTRESS TILTYARD
    In troth sister, I hope you will do well for all this.
MISTRESS GALLIPOT
    I hope I shall: farewell good sister: sweet Master Goshawk.   185
MASTER GALLIPOT
    Welcome brother, most kindly welcome sir.
OMNES
    Thanks, sir, for our good cheer.

                            Exeunt all but GALLIPOT *and his wife*

MASTER GALLIPOT
    It shall be so; because a crafty knave
    Shall not outreach me, nor walk by my door
    With my wife arm in arm, as 'twere his whore,   190
    I'll give him a golden coxcomb; thirty pound,
    Tush Pru, what's thirty pound? Sweet duck, look cheerly.

174–5 *feeds … abroad* a common phrase for marital unfaithfulness
174 *mutton* food for lust, hence prostitutes
176–7 *at rack and manger* i.e. at his 'food'. To live at rack and manger was to live in
    reckless abundance. Cf. Wyclif, *Works*, 435 (qu. *Oxf. Dict. English Proverbs*,
    661): 'it is yuel to kepe a wast hors in stable … but it is worse to have a woman
    at racke and at manger'.
178 *saddle him in's kind* use him according to the man he is, do by him as he does by
    me (picking up Goshawk's submerged metaphor)
179 *ride our journey* enjoy our sexual pleasure
182 *amble* originally used only of horses; the whole sentence continues the sexual
    punning
188 *because* to the end that

MISTRESS GALLIPOT

Thou art worthy of my heart, thou buy'st it dearly.

Enter LAXTON *muffled*

LAXTON

Uds light, the tide's against me, a pox of your pothecary-
ship: oh for some glister to set him going; 'tis one of   195
Hercules' labours to tread one of these city hens, because
their cocks are still crowing over them; there's no turning
tail here, I must on.

MISTRESS GALLIPOT

Oh husband see, he comes.

MASTER GALLIPOT

Let me deal with him.   200

LAXTON

Bless you, sir.

MASTER GALLIPOT

Be you blest too, sir, if you come in peace.

LAXTON

Have you any good pudding tobacco, sir?

MISTRESS GALLIPOT

Oh pick no quarrels, gentle sir, my husband
Is not a man of weapon, as you are,   205
He knows all, I have opened all before him
Concerning you.

LAXTON [*Aside*]   Zounds, has she shown my letters?

MISTRESS GALLIPOT

Suppose my case were yours, what would you do
At such a pinch, such batteries, such assaults,
Of father, mother, kindred, to dissolve   210
The knot you tied, and to be bound to him?
How could you shift this storm off?

LAXTON   If I know, hang me.

MISTRESS GALLIPOT

Besides, a story of your death was read
Each minute to me.

---

195 *glister* an old form of 'clyster', an enema. The word was used contemptuously of
doctors and apothecaries (as in the character name of the quack in *A Family of
Love*).

197 *still* always

203 *pudding tobacco* compressed tobacco made into rolls resembling a pudding or
sausage; but the threat in Laxton's words which Mistress Gallipot recognises
probably comes from the suggestion that he is after Gallipot's pudding or guts

LAXTON [*Aside*]   What a pox means this riddling?
MASTER GALLIPOT
    Be wise, sir, let not you and I be tossed   215
    On lawyers' pens; they have sharp nibs and draw
    Men's very heart-blood from them; what need you, sir,
    To beat the drum of my wife's infamy,
    And call your friends together, sir, to prove
    Your precontract, when sh'has confessed it?
LAXTON   Hm sir,   220
    Has she confessed it?
MASTER GALLIPOT   Sh'has, faith, to me, sir,
    Upon your letter sending.
MISTRESS GALLIPOT   I have, I have.
LAXTON
    [*Aside*] If I let this iron cool, call me slave.
    – Do you hear, you dame Prudence? Think'st thou, vile
      woman,   225
    I'll take these blows and wink?
MISTRESS GALLIPOT   Upon my knees –
LAXTON
    Out, impudence.
MASTER GALLIPOT   Good sir –
LAXTON   You goatish slaves,
    No wild fowl to cut up but mine?
MASTER GALLIPOT   Alas sir,
    You make her flesh to tremble: fright her not,
    She shall do reason, and what's fit.
LAXTON   I'll have thee,   230
    Wert thou more common than an hospital,
    And more diseased.
MASTER GALLIPOT   But one word, good sir.
LAXTON   So, sir.
MASTER GALLIPOT
    I married her, have lien with her, and got
    Two children on her body, think but on that;
    Have you so beggarly an appetite   235

---

215 *tossed* bandied, made the subject of talk
220 *precontract* ed. (precontact Q) cf. above, l. 117n.
228 ' "To cut up wild fowl" was a cant expression, the meaning of which is suffi-
    ciently obvious' (Bullen). It seems, however, not to be recorded in *OED* or in
    contemporary canting dictionaries. But cf. Webster, *The White Devil*, II.i.90–2:
    'We fear / When Tiber to each prowling passenger / Discovers flocks of wild
    ducks...' and *Cymbeline*, I.iv.89: 'strange fowl light upon neighboring ponds'.
231 *common* open to all comers; cf. III.i.135

When I upon a dainty dish have fed
To dine upon my scraps, my leavings? Ha, sir?
Do I come near you now, sir?
LAXTON   Be-Lady, you touch me.
MASTER GALLIPOT
Would not you scorn to wear my clothes, sir?
LAXTON   Right, sir.
MASTER GALLIPOT
Then pray, sir, wear not her, for she's a garment   240
So fitting for my body, I'm loath
Another should put it on, you will undo both.
Your letter (as she said) complained you had spent
In quest of her some thirty pound, I'll pay it;
Shall that, sir, stop this gap up 'twixt you two?   245
LAXTON
Well, if I swallow this wrong, let her thank you:
The money being paid, sir, I am gone;
Farewell: oh women! Happy's he trusts none.
MISTRESS GALLIPOT
Dispatch him hence, sweet husband.
MASTER GALLIPOT   Yes, dear wife:
Pray sir, come in: ere Master Laxton part   250
Thou shalt in wine drink to him.
MISTRESS GALLIPOT   With all my heart.

                    Exit MASTER GALLIPOT

– How dost thou like my wit?
LAXTON   Rarely: that wile
By which the serpent did the first woman beguile
Did ever since all women's bosoms fill;
Y'are apple-eaters all, deceivers still.   [*Exeunt*] 255

236 *a dainty dish* Cf. the modern slang 'dish' for an attractive girl.
238 *now* ed. (uow Q)
        Be-Lady a corruption of 'By our Lady'
251 sd *Exit* MASTER GALLIPOT ed. (Exit Maister Gallipot and his wife Q)
255 sd *Exeunt* ed. (Exit Laxton Q)

[Act III, Scene iii]

Enter SIR ALEXANDER WENGRAVE, SIR DAVY DAPPER,
SIR ADAM APPLETON *at one door, and* TRAPDOOR *at
another door*

SIR ALEXANDER
Out with your tale, Sir Davy, to Sir Adam:
A knave is in mine eye deep in my debt.
SIR DAVY
Nay: if he be a knave, sir, hold him fast.

[SIR DAVY *and* SIR ADAM *talk apart*]

SIR ALEXANDER
Speak softly, what egg is there hatching now?
TRAPDOOR
A duck's egg, sir, a duck that has eaten a frog. I have   5
cracked the shell, and some villainy or other will peep out
presently; the duck that sits is the bouncing ramp, that
roaring girl my mistress, the drake that must tread is your
son Sebastian.
SIR ALEXANDER
Be quick.   10
TRAPDOOR
As the tongue of an oyster-wench.
SIR ALEXANDER
And see thy news be true.
TRAPDOOR
As a barber's every Saturday night. Mad Moll –
SIR ALEXANDER
Ah.
TRAPDOOR
Must be let in without knocking at your back gate.   15
SIR ALEXANDER
So.
TRAPDOOR
Your chamber will be made bawdy.

---

0 sd 2–3 *at one door . . . at another door* i.e. of the stage: the setting is in fact a street
2 *A knave . . . debt* i.e. I have caught sight of a knave who is in my debt
5 *a duck that has eaten a frog* The phrase seems to have no more specific meaning
   than an allusion to the villainy that Trapdoor goes on to speak about.
7 *bouncing ramp* rampant, wanton creature
13 *As a barber's* Barbers are well placed to hear gossip.

SIR ALEXANDER
  Good.
TRAPDOOR
  She comes in a shirt of male.
SIR ALEXANDER
  How, shirt of mail?   20
TRAPDOOR
  Yes sir, or a male shirt, that's to say in man's apparel.
SIR ALEXANDER
  To my son?
TRAPDOOR
  Close to your son: your son and her moon will be in con-
  junction, if all almanacs lie not: her black saveguard is
  turned into a deep slop, the holes of her upper body to   25
  button-holes, her waistcoat to a doublet, her placket to the
  ancient seat of a codpiece, and you shall take 'em both
  with standing collars.
SIR ALEXANDER
  Art sure of this?
TRAPDOOR
  As every throng is sure of a pickpocket, as sure as a whore   30
  is of the clients all Michaelmas Term, and of the pox after
  the term.

23-4 *in conjunction* Two planets were said to be in conjunction when they were in
      the same sign of the zodiac (their influences were then thought to reinforce one
      another); the moon is in conjunction with the sun at new moon. But 'conjunc-
      tion' was also commonly used for copulation.
24   *saveguard* See II.i.161 sd and n.
25   *slop* See II.ii.81–2 and n.
     holes of her upper body 'Hole' has various low sexual uses and here possibly sug-
     gests nipples. But 'body' (of which 'bodice' is a variant form of the plural) was
     regularly used for the part of a woman's dress above the waist, which would
     commonly be laced through a series of holes. Cf. *A Mad World, My Masters*,
     III.iii.100.
26   *waistcoat* In the sixteenth and early seventeenth centuries elaborate waistcoats
     were fashionable. They were worn beneath an outer gown, but so as to be seen.
     placket the opening or slit at the top of a skirt or petticoat (constantly, like 'cod-
     piece', with sexual associations)
28   *standing collars* Upstanding collars became fashionable for men in the early sev-
     enteenth century: see the illustration on the title-page. There is probably a play
     on 'stand' in the sense of an erection (cf. I.ii.56–7n.) and conceivably a hint of
     some contraceptive device.
31   *Michaelmas Term* the first term of the legal year, when the termers will have
     plenty of money

SIR ALEXANDER
The time of their tilting?
TRAPDOOR
Three.
SIR ALEXANDER
The day?   35
TRAPDOOR
This.
SIR ALEXANDER
Away, ply it, watch her.
TRAPDOOR
As the devil doth for the death of a bawd, I'll watch her,
do you catch her.
SIR ALEXANDER
She's fast: here weave thou the nets, hark.   40
TRAPDOOR
They are made.
SIR ALEXANDER
I told them thou didst owe me money; hold it up: main-
tain't.
TRAPDOOR
Stiffly, as a puritan does contention; – Fox, I owe thee not
the value of a halfpenny halter.   [*Angrily, as in a quarrel*]   45
SIR ALEXANDER
Thou shalt be hanged in't ere thou scape so. Varlet, I'll
make thee look through a grate.
TRAPDOOR
I'll do't presently, through a tavern grate. Drawer! Pish.

Exit

SIR ADAM
Has the knave vexed you, sir?
SIR ALEXANDER   Asked him my money,
He swears my son received it: oh that boy   50
Will ne'er leave heaping sorrows on my heart,
Till he has broke it quite.
SIR ADAM   Is he still wild?
SIR ALEXANDER
As is a Russian bear.

42 *them* i.e. the other knights
   hold it up i.e. the pretence
47 *grate* prison grating
48 *Drawer!* He calls offstage as to a drawer in the tavern.

SIR ADAM   But he has left
His old haunt with that baggage?
SIR ALEXANDER   Worse still and worse,
He lays on me his shame, I on him my curse.
SIR DAVY
My son Jack Dapper then shall run with him,   55
All in one pasture.
SIR ADAM   Proves your son bad too, sir?
SIR DAVY
As villainy can make him: your Sebastian
Doats but on one drab, mine on a thousand,
A noise of fiddlers, tobacco, wine, and a whore,
A mercer that will let him take up more,
Dice, and a water-spaniel with a duck: oh,   60
Bring him abed with these, when his purse jingles,
Roaring boys follow at's tail, fencers and ningles
(Beasts Adam ne'er gave name to), these horse-leeches
    suck
My son: he being drawn dry, they all live on smoke.
SIR ALEXANDER   65
Tobacco?
SIR DAVY   Right: but I have in my brain
A windmill going that shall grind to dust
The follies of my son, and make him wise,
Or a stark fool; pray lend me your advice.
BOTH
That shall you, good Sir Davy.   70
SIR DAVY   Here's the springe
I ha' set to catch this woodcock in: an action
In a false name (unknown to him) is entered

---

53 *Russian bear* Cf. *Macbeth*, III.iv.99 ('the rugged Russian bear'). Bears were im-
   ported from Russia for baiting, and their fierceness became proverbial.
60 *noise* band of musicians (not necessarily contemptuously)
61 *take up* i.e. on credit
64 *fencers* swordsmen   *ningles* (or ingles) boy-favourites, catamites
65 *horse-leeches* farriers (alternatively a large variety of leech), widely used as a contemptuous term for rapacious parasites: cf. *A Fair Quarrel*, III.ii.170
67 *Tobacco* The popularity of smoking by the early years of James I's reign is evi-
   denced by Barnabe Riche's estimate that there were then at least seven thousand
   tobacco shops in London: annual takings were said to be over £300,000.
68 *windmill* picking up the implied image of a tobacco-mill
70 *advice* ed. (advise Q). Q spelling gives a perfect rhyme.
71–2 *the springe ... to catch this woodcock* Probably a direct theft from *Hamlet*,
   I.iv.115, which seems to be the first recorded instance of the figurative use of this
   phrase, though 'woodcock' was in common use for simpleton. Cf. also *Twelfth
   Night*, II.v.84.

I'th'counter to arrest Jack Dapper.
BOTH   Ha, ha, he.
SIR DAVY
    Think you the counter cannot break him?
SIR ADAM   Break him?
    Yes and break's heart too if he lie there long.
SIR DAVY   75
    I'll make him sing a counter-tenor sure.
SIR ADAM
    No way to tame him like it, there he shall learn
    What money is indeed, and how to spend it.
SIR DAVY
    He's bridled there.
SIR ALEXANDER   Ay, yet knows not how to mend it:
    Bedlam cures not more madmen in a year
    Than one of the counters does: men pay more dear   80
    There for their wit than anywhere; a counter,
    Why 'tis a university, who not sees?
    As scholars there, so here men take degrees,
    And follow the same studies all alike.
    Scholars learn first logic and rhetoric,   85
    So does a prisoner; with fine honey'd speech
    At's first coming in he doth persuade, beseech
    He may be lodged with one that is not itchy,
    To lie in a clean chamber, in sheets not lousy;
    But when he has no money, then does he try   90
    By subtle logic and quaint sophistry
    To make the keeper trust him.

---

74 *counter* the mayor's court or hall of justice, to which a debtor's prison was at-
    tached; also written 'compter'
77 *counter-tenor* a high male alto. Sir Davy suggests that he would like to geld his
    son as well as have him locked away.
80 *bridled* with a quibble on Bridewell, already a common term for a house of cor-
    rection
84 *a university* Middleton was fond of this joke. Cf. *The Phoenix*, IV.iii.19 and
    Michaelmas Term, III.iv.83ff.: 'H'as at least sixteen at this instant proceeded in
    both the Counters: some bach'lors, some masters, some doctors of captivity.' Sir
    Thomas Overbury in 1613 called a prison 'an university of poor scholars, in
    which three arts are chiefly studied; to pray, to curse, and to write letters'. The
    joke survived until the nineteenth century when the Marshalsea was still known
    as the college, as in *Little Dorrit*. Dekker had personal experience of the counter.
87 *logic and rhetoric* From the foundation of the universities logic was regarded
    as the science of sciences, and both these subjects held a principal place in the
    curricula of the English universities until the middle of the seventeenth century.

SIR ADAM   Say they do?
SIR ALEXANDER
  Then he's a graduate.
SIR DAVY   Say they trust him not?   95
SIR ALEXANDER
  Then is he held a freshman and a sot,
  And never shall commence, but, being still barred,
  Be expulsed from the master's side, to th' twopenny ward,
  Or else i'th'Hole be placed.
SIR ADAM   When then, I pray,
  Proceeds a prisoner?
SIR ALEXANDER   When, money being the theme,   100
  He can dispute with his hard creditors' hearts,
  And get out clear, he's then a Master of Arts.
  Sir Davy, send your son to Wood Street College,
  A gentleman can nowhere get more knowledge.
SIR DAVY
  There gallants study hard.
SIR ALEXANDER   True: to get money.   105
SIR DAVY
  'Lies by th' heels i'faith: thanks, thanks, I ha' sent
  For a couple of bears shall paw him.

              Enter SERGEANT CURTILAX *and* YEOMAN HANGER

SIR ADAM   Who comes yonder?
SIR DAVY
  They look like puttocks, these should be they.

---

97 *commence* be admitted to a degree
98 *the master's side* The governor of a prison was allowed to let certain rooms for his
    own profit; these were, of course, the best in the prison. The twopenny ward (cf.
    Chapman, et al., *Eastward Ho!*, V.ii.61) may be the mistress's side referred to in
    The Phoenix (IV.iii.22). The poorest prisoners were confined in the 'Hole', a
    name specially given to the worst dungeon in the Wood Street Counter.
99 *be placed* ed. (E.C.) (beg plac'd Q; beg place *Gomme*)
100 *Proceeds* advances from B.A. to a higher degree
101 *dispute* One proved one's right to proceed by engaging in a *disputatio*, in which
    parties formally sustain, attack, or defend a given question or thesis. There is a
    brief parody of a disputation in *A Chaste Maid in Cheapside*, IV.i.
103 *Wood Street College* Cf. above, l. 84 and n. Conditions in Wood Street Counter,
    which stood on the east side of the street near the junction with Gresham Street,
    seem to have been particularly bad even by the standards of the early seven-
    teenth century (cf. *Sh. Eng.*, II, 508).
106 *'Lies by th' heels* (i.e. he lies) he is being arrested (or put in irons)
107 *bears* rough fellows; cf. 'boys more tough than bears' (*The Honest Whore*, part 1,
    IV.iii.99)
108 *puttocks* kites, applied opprobriously to catchpolls

SIR ALEXANDER   I know 'em,
They are officers: sir, we'll leave you.
SIR DAVY   My good knights,
Leave me, you see I'm haunted now with spirits.   110
BOTH
Fare you well, sir.

Exeunt [SIR] ALEX[ANDER] *and* [SIR] ADAM

CURTILAX
This old muzzle-chops should be he by the fellow's de-
scription: – save you, sir.
SIR DAVY
Come hither, you mad varlets, did not my man tell you I
watched here for you?   115
CURTILAX
One in a blue coat, sir, told us, that in this place an old
gentleman would watch for us, a thing contrary to our
oath, for we are to watch for every wicked member in a
city.
SIR DAVY
You'll watch then for ten thousand, what's thy name hon-   120
esty?
CURTILAX
Sergeant Curtilax I, sir.
SIR DAVY
An excellent name for a sergeant, Curtilax.
Sergeants indeed are weapons of the law:
When prodigal ruffians far in debt are grown,   125
Should not you cut them, citizens were o'erthrown.
Thou dwell'st hereby in Holborn, Curtilax?
CURTILAX
That's my circuit, sir, I conjure most in that circle.
SIR DAVY
And what young toward whelp is this?

---

110 *spirits* kidnappers or abductors, with of course a play on the common sense
116 *One in a blue coat* This was the traditional dress of a servant until the early sev-
     enteenth century.
120–1 *honesty* i.e. honest fellow
122 *Curtilax* a much perverted form of 'cutlass', which became so distinct that it ac-
     quired a kind of permanent standing, the identification of the final part with 'ax'
     being favoured by the use of the weapon in delivering slashing blows (*OED*)
129 *toward* promising, hopeful

HANGER
  Of the same litter, his yeoman, sir, my name's Hanger.   130
SIR DAVY
  Yeoman Hanger:
  One pair of shears sure cut out both your coats,
  You have two names most dangerous to men's throats,
  You two are villainous loads on gentlemen's backs,
  Dear ware, this Hanger and this Curtilax.   135
CURTILAX
  We are as other men are, sir, I cannot see but he who
  makes a show of honesty and religion, if his claws can fas-
  ten to his liking, he draws blood; all that live in the world
  are but great fish and little fish, and feed upon one
  another, some eat up whole men, a sergeant cares but for   140
  the shoulder of a man; they call us knaves and curs, but
  many times he that sets us on worries more lambs one year
  than we do in seven.
SIR DAVY
  Spoke like a noble Cerberus: is the action entered?
HANGER
  His name is entered in the book of unbelievers.   145
SIR DAVY
  What book's that?
CURTILAX
  The book where all prisoners' names stand, and not one
  amongst forty, when he comes in, believes to come out in
  haste.
SIR DAVY
  Be as dogged to him as your office allows you to be.   150
BOTH
  Oh sir.
SIR DAVY
  You know the unthrift Jack Dapper?

---

130 *yeoman* an assistant to an official, but also a servant subordinate to a sergeant
132 *One pair of shears ... both your coats* i.e. you are two of a kind. 'There went but
    a pair of shears between them' was a common proverbial expression: cf. *Measure
    for Measure*, I.ii.27.
135 *ware* The word was sometimes used for textiles; the image is hardly precise.
139 *great fish and little fish* 'The great fish eat up the small' was a bitter proverbial jest
    of constant application. Cf. *Pericles*, II.i.26–9: 'Master, I marvel how the fishes
    live in the sea. / Why, as men do a-land; the great ones eat up the little ones.'
140–1 *for the shoulder of a man* because he apprehends men by catching hold of their
    shoulders
144 *Cerberus* Cf. III.i.23 n.; *dogged* in l. 150 plays on this.

CURTILAX

Ay, ay, sir, that gull? As well as I know my yeoman.

SIR DAVY

And you know his father too, Sir Davy Dapper?

CURTILAX

As damned a usurer as ever was among Jews; if he were   155
sure his father's skin would yield him any money, he
would when he dies flay it off, and sell it to cover drums
for children at Bartholomew Fair.

SIR DAVY

[*Aside*] What toads are these to spit poison on a man to his
face! – Do you see, my honest rascals? Yonder greyhound   160
is the dog he hunts with, out of that tavern Jack Dapper
will sally: sa, sa; give the counter, on, set upon him.

BOTH

We'll charge him upo'th'back, sir.

SIR DAVY

Take no bail, put mace enough into his caudle, double
your files, traverse your ground.   165

BOTH

Brave, sir.

SIR DAVY

Cry arm, arm, arm.

BOTH

Thus, sir.

SIR DAVY

There boy, there boy, away: look to your prey, my true
English wolves, and – and so I vanish.   *Exit*   170

---

157 *flay* ed. (flea Q)

158 *Bartholomew Fair* had by this time grown to enormous size, incorporating four
parishes and lasting for a fortnight from 23 August (St Bartholomew's Eve),
when it was opened by the Lord Mayor. It was the Londoner's great annual jam-
boree, and amongst other things, the chief national cloth sale.

162 *sa, sa* in hunting, a call to attention
give the counter To hunt counter is to run a false scent, or follow it in reverse direction; so here, turn him back. There is doubtless a play on counter in the sense
of prison (cf. above, ll. 74ff.).

164 *mace* Sergeants carried maces; *caudle* is gruel mixed with spiced ale, for which
mace would be a regular ingredient. The same jest appears in *A Mad World, My
Masters*, III.ii.69.

164–5 *double your files, travers your ground* literally, make the ranks smaller by putting
two files in one, move from side to side; but Sir Davy is presumably just being
briskly military, using at random the terms he knows

CURTILAX

Some warden of the sergeants begat this old fellow, upon
my life: stand close.

HANGER

Shall the ambuscado lie in one place?

CURTILAX

No, nook thou yonder.

Enter MOLL *and* TRAPDOOR

MOLL

Ralph.   175

TRAPDOOR

What says my brave captain male and female?

MOLL

This Holborn is such a wrangling street.

TRAPDOOR

That's because lawyers walks to and fro in't.

MOLL

Here's such jostling, as if everyone we met were drunk and
reeled.   180

TRAPDOOR

Stand, mistress, do you not smell carrion?

MOLL

Carrion? No, yet I spy ravens.

TRAPDOOR

Some poor wind-shaken gallant will anon fall into sore
labour, and these men-midwives must bring him to bed

---

171 *Some warden of the sergeants* one, that is, crabbed enough to be in charge of
sergeants

173 *ambuscado* ambush, a common seventeenth-century form used especially of the
force employed

174 *nook thou yonder* ed. (uooke Q) hide in that nook

177 *wrangling* noisy, disputatious

178 Several Inns of Court stood in Holborn, then as now the principal east–west
street in the northern part of the City.

181 *carrion* A carrion or carren doe was one which was pregnant (cf. Gascoigne,
Woodmanship, p. 5); hence the quibbles in Trapdoor's next speech. Ravens are
carrion-eaters (in the more familiar sense), but 'raven' or 'ravin' also means rob-
bery or rapine. The complex joke is now irrecoverable without much labour.

183 *wind-shaken* weakened or flawed at heart as timber supposed cracked by force of
the wind

184 *men-midwives* another well-used joke; cf. *The Whore of Babylon*, II.i.61ff.: 'Do
you not know (mistress) what Sergeants are? ... why they are certain men-midwives, that never bring people to bed, but when they are sore in labour, that nobody else can deliver them.' And see Jonson, *The Staple of News*, ind. 43ff. and
Field, *Amends for Ladies*, IV.i.164f.

i'the counter, there all those that are great with child with   185
debts lie in.

MOLL

Stand up.

TRAPDOOR

Like your new maypole.

HANGER

Whist, whew.

CURTILAX

Hump, no.   190

MOLL

Peeping? It shall go hard, huntsmen, but I'll spoil your
game: they look for all the world like two infected maltmen
coming muffled up in their cloaks in a frosty morning to
London.

TRAPDOOR

A course, captain; a bear comes to the stake.   195

Enter JACK DAPPER *and* GULL

MOLL

It should be so, for the dogs struggle to be let loose.

HANGER

Whew.

CURTILAX

Hemp.

MOLL

Hark Trapdoor, follow your leader.

JACK DAPPER

Gull.   200

GULL

Master.

JACK DAPPER

Didst ever see such an ass as I am, boy?

GULL

No by my troth, sir, to lose all your money, yet have false
dice of your own, why 'tis as I saw a great fellow used

---

189 *Whist* Hanger whistles questioningly to Curtilax; *whew* is likewise a whistle, but
also a verb meaning to move sharply.

192 *two infected maltmen* Mulholland (p. 171) quotes F. P. Wilson, *The Plague in
Shakespeare's London*, Oxford, 1963, p. 36: 'In 1630 it came to the notice of the
Privy Council that those who carried malt into the City were accustomed to return home with rags "for manuring of the soiling of the ground" and the practice was forbidden.' This practice would have made maltmen particularly sus-
ceptible to infection.

195 *course* the animal pursued (*OED* 7b)

t'other day, he had a fair sword and buckler, and yet a 205
butcher dry-beat him with a cudgel.

MOLL AND TRAPDOOR

Honest servant, fly; fly, Master Dapper, you'll be arrested
else.

JACK DAPPER

Run, Gull, and draw.

GULL

Run, master, Gull follows you.   210

Exeunt [JACK] DAPPER *and* GULL

CURTILAX

I know you well enough, you're but a whore to hang upon
any man.

MOLL

Whores then are like sergeants, so now hang you; – draw,
rogue, but strike not: for a broken pate they'll keep their
beds, and recover twenty marks damages.   215

CURTILAX

You shall pay for this rescue; – run down Shoe Lane and
meet him.

TRAPDOOR

Shoo, is this a rescue, gentlemen, or no?

MOLL

Rescue? A pox on 'em, Trapdoor, let's away,
I'm glad I have done perfect one good work today;   220
If any gentleman be in scrivener's bands,
Send but for Moll, she'll bail him by these hands.

Exeunt

206 *dry-beat* beat soundly (with 'dry blows', i.e. those not drawing blood)
207 sp MOLL AND TRAPDOOR ed. (Both Q): perhaps the speech should be divided between the two.
    servant ed. (Serieant Q corr.: Seriant Q uncorr.) I follow Dyce and Bullen.
Bowers reads 'Sir' on the grounds that Gull would not be referred to before his
master, and thinks the compositor may have mistakenly expanded the abbrevi-
ation 'Sᵊ'. That would be an odd mistake; and who would call Jack Dapper
'Honest Sir'? Mulholland retains 'Sergeant' on the grounds that 'stage business
of some sort could clear up the difficulty'.
210 Bullen suggests that Moll holds Curtilax at this point.   214 *rogue* i.e. Trapdoor
215 *twenty marks* The mark was worth two-thirds of a pound.
216 *rescue* the forcible taking of a person or goods out of custody – a very serious offence. Cf. *Coriolanus*, III.i.275, and *The Honest Whore*, part 1, IV.iii.141: 'A rescue, prentices, my master's catchpolled'.
    Shoe Lane (now bridged by Holborn Viaduct) ran down from Holborn towards
Fleet Street and the Bridewell.
221 *scrivener* in the general sense of notary

[Act IV, Scene i]

Enter SIR ALEXANDER WENGRAVE *solus*

SIR ALEXANDER
Unhappy in the follies of a son
Led against judgment, sense, obedience,
And all the powers of nobleness and wit;

Enter TRAPDOOR

Oh wretched father. – Now Trapdoor, will she come?
TRAPDOOR
In man's apparel, sir, I am in her heart now,   5
And share in all her secrets.
SIR ALEXANDER   Peace, peace, peace.
Here, take my German watch, hang't up in sight,
That I may see her hang in English for't.
TRAPDOOR
I warrant you for that now, next sessions rids her, sir, this
watch will bring her in better than a hundred constables.   10
SIR ALEXANDER
Good Trapdoor, sayst thou so? Thou cheer'st my heart
After a storm of sorrow, – my gold chain, too,
Here, take a hundred marks in yellow links.
TRAPDOOR
That will do well to bring the watch to light, sir:
And worth a thousand of your headborough's lanthorns.   15
SIR ALEXANDER
Place that o'the court cupboard, let it lie
Full in the view of her thief-whorish eye.
TRAPDOOR
She cannot miss it, sir, I see't so plain
That I could steal't myself.
SIR ALEXANDER   Perhaps thou shalt too,

---

7 *my German watch* Allusions to German watches and clocks are frequent in plays
of this period. Cf., e.g., *Love's Labour's Lost*, III.i.190, and *A Mad World, My
Masters*, IV.i.21. They were renowned for their complexity and ingenuity.
9 *sessions* i.e. of court
13 *a hundred marks in yellow links* i.e. his chain of office as magistrate. Sir Bounteous
Progress is cheated of an identical one in *A Mad World, My Masters* (V.i.122 and
V.ii.170), where Follywit (disguised as a player) asks for a chain to serve for a
justice's hat.
15 *headborough* constable
16 *court cupboard* a form of sideboard consisting normally of three shelves supported
on elaborately carved legs

That or something as weighty; what she leaves,   20
Thou shalt come closely in, and filch away,
And all the weight upon her back I'll lay.

TRAPDOOR

You cannot assure that, sir.

SIR ALEXANDER   No? What lets it?

TRAPDOOR

Being a stout girl, perhaps she'll desire pressing,
Then all the weight must lie upon her belly.   25

SIR ALEXANDER

Belly or back I care not so I've one.

TRAPDOOR

You're of my mind for that, sir.

SIR ALEXANDER

Hang up my ruff-band with the diamond at it,
It may be she'll like that best.

TRAPDOOR

[*Aside*] It's well for her that she must have her choice, he   30
thinks nothing too good for her. – If you hold on this mind
a little longer, it shall be the first work I do to turn thief
myself; would do a man good to be hanged when he is so
well provided for.

SIR ALEXANDER

So, well said; all hangs well, would she hung so too,   35
The sight would please me more than all their glisterings:
Oh that my mysteries to such straits should run,
That I must rob myself to bless my son.   *Exeunt*

       Enter SEBASTIAN, *with* MARY FITZ-ALLARD *like a page,*
             and MOLL [*in man's clothes*]

SEBASTIAN

Thou hast done me a kind office, without touch
Either of sin or shame, our loves are honest.   40

MOLL

I'd scorn to make such shift to bring you together else.

SEBASTIAN

Now have I time and opportunity
Without all fear to bid thee welcome, love.   *Kiss*

MARY

Never with more desire and harder venture.

---

21 *closely* secretly
23 *lets* prevents
36 *glisterings* ed. (gilsterings Q)
37 *mysteries* cunning

MOLL
How strange this shows, one man to kiss another.   45
SEBASTIAN
I'd kiss such men to choose, Moll,
Methinks a woman's lip tastes well in a doublet.
MOLL
Many an old madam has the better fortune then,
Whose breaths grew stale before the fashion came:
If that will help 'em, as you think 'twill do,   50
They'll learn in time to pluck on the hose too.
SEBASTIAN
The older they wax, Moll – troth I speak seriously,
As some have a conceit their drink tastes better
In an outlandish cup than in our own,
So methinks every kiss she gives me now   55
In this strange form, is worth a pair of two.
Here we are safe, and furthest from the eye
Of all suspicion, this is my father's chamber,
Upon which floor he never steps till night.
Here he mistrusts me not, nor I his coming;   60
At mine own chamber he still pries unto me,
My freedom is not there at mine own finding,
Still checked and curbed; here he shall miss his purpose.
MOLL
And what's your business, now you have your mind, sir?
At your great suit I promised you to come,   65
I pitied her for name's sake, that a Moll
Should be so crossed in love when there's so many
That owes nine lays apiece, and not so little:
My tailor fitted her, how like you his work?
SEBASTIAN
So well, no art can mend it for this purpose;   70
But to thy wit and help we're chief in debt,

46 *to choose* for choice
48 *Many an old madam* Doublets were occasionally worn by women (without the
    pretence of being dressed as men), but whether especially by bawds seems un-
    recorded.
56 *pair of two* This has sometimes been amended to 'pair or two'; but 'pair' could
    mean a set of indeterminate number, and I have occasionally heard 'pair of two'
    in colloquial speech quite recently. The amendment somewhat weakens
    Sebastian's gesture.
58 *father's* ed. (fathets Q)
61 *still* always
64 *business, now* ed. (business now, Q)
68 *lays* Bullen glosses 'wagers', but a sexual meaning seems more likely.

And must live still beholding.

MOLL   Any honest pity
I'm willing to bestow upon poor ring-doves.

SEBASTIAN
I'll offer no worse play.

MOLL   Nay, and you should, sir,
I should draw first and prove the quicker man.   75

SEBASTIAN
Hold, there shall need no weapon at this meeting,
But 'cause thou shalt not loose thy fury idle,
Here take this viol, run upon the guts,
And end thy quarrel singing.

MOLL   Like a swan above bridge,
For look you here's the bridge, and here am I.   80

SEBASTIAN
Hold on, sweet Moll.

MARY
I've heard her much commended, sir, for one that was
ne'er taught.

MOLL
I'm much beholding to 'em: well since you'll needs put us
together, sir, I'll play my part as well as I can: it shall ne'er   85
be said I came into a gentleman's chamber and let his instrument hang by the walls.

SEBASTIAN
Why well said, Moll, i'faith, it had been a shame for that
gentleman then, that would have let it hung still and ne'er
offered thee it.   90

MOLL
There it should have been still then for Moll, for though
the world judge impudently of me, I ne'er came into that
chamber yet where I took down the instrument myself.

SEBASTIAN
Pish, let 'em prate abroad, th'art here where thou art
known and loved: there be a thousand close dames that   95
will call the viol an unmannerly instrument for a woman,

---

77 *'cause thou shalt not loose thy fury idle* There is probably a play here on 'fury' in
   the sense of (musical) inspiration. Cf. Morley, *Introduction to Music* (1597),
   p. 35: 'This hath been a mighty musical fury, which hath caused him to show
   such diversity in so small bounds.' Thus, 'so that your passion is not wasted'.
79 *a swan above bridge* Swans were plentiful in the London reaches of the Thames.
80 *bridge* i.e. of the violin

and therefore talk broadly of thee, when you shall have
them sit wider to a worse quality.

MOLL
Push, I ever fall asleep and think not of 'em, sir, and thus
I dream.   100

SEBASTIAN
Prithee let's hear thy dream, Moll.

MOLL
      I dream there is a mistress,   *The song*
        And she lays out the money,
      She goes unto her sisters,
        She never comes at any.   105

        Enter SIR ALEXANDER *behind them*

      She says she went to the Burse for patterns,
      You shall find her at Saint Kathern's,
      And comes home with never a penny.

SEBASTIAN
That's a free mistress, faith.

SIR ALEXANDER
[*Aside*] Ay, ay, ay, like her that sings it, one of thine own   110
choosing.

MOLL
But shall I dream again?
      Here comes a wench will brave ye,
        Her courage was so great,
      She lay with one o' the navy,   115
        Her husband lying i'the Fleet.
      Yet oft with him she cavilled,
        I wonder what she ails,
      Her husband's ship lay gravelled,

97–8 *when you shall have them sit wider* The instrument is a gamba, played at this
    period with the body of the viol gripped between the player's thighs or knees (cf.
    A Trick to Catch the Old One, I.i.133); the sexual punning on 'instrument'
    reaches its home in this line.

106 *the Burse* probably an allusion to the Royal Exchange, built (on the site in
    Cornhill) by Sir Thomas Gresham in 1567. See *A Chaste Maid*, I.ii.34: 'As if she
    lay with all the gaudy shops / In Gresham's Burse about her'.

107 *Saint Kathern's* perhaps an allusion to St Katherine's Fair, which, until the late
    sixteenth century, had been held to provide funds for St Katherine's Hospital on
    Tower Hill. The hospital precinct had a prison called St Katherine's Hole. The
    whole area had by the seventeenth century a generally bad reputation. In *The
    Alchemist* (V.iii.55f.) St Kathern's is said to be 'where they use to keep / The bet-
    ter sort of mad folks'.

116 *i'the Fleet* i.e. in the prison

When hers could hoise up sails,   120
Yet she began like all my foes
To call whore first: for so do those,
A pox of all false tails.

SEBASTIAN
Marry, amen say I.

SIR ALEXANDER
So say I too.   125

MOLL
Hang up the viol now, sir: all this while I was in a dream,
one shall lie rudely then; but being awake, I keep my legs
together. A watch, what's o'clock here?

SIR ALEXANDER
Now, now she's trapped.

MOLL
Between one and two: nay then I care not: a watch and a   130
musician are cousin-germans in one thing, they must both
keep time well, or there's no goodness in 'em; the one else
deserves to be dashed against a wall, and t'other to have
his brains knocked out with a fiddle case. What, a loose
chain and a dangling diamond? Here were a brave booty   135
for an evening-thief now, there's many a younger brother
would be glad to look twice in at a window for't, and wrig-
gle in and out like an eel in a sandbag. Oh, if men's secret
youthful faults should judge 'em, 'twould be the general'st
execution that ere was seen in England; there would be but 140
few left to sing the ballets, there would be so much work:
most of our brokers would be chosen for hangmen, a good
day for them: they might renew their wardropes of free
cost then.

SEBASTIAN
This is the roaring wench must do us good.   145

---

123 *tails* cant term for sexual organs and so extended to their owners; here with a
   play on 'tales'
131 *cousin-germans* first cousins. The watch is German.
134–40 prose ed. (*arranged as rough verse* Q).
138 *like an eel in a sandbag* a proverbial phrase used of things languishing for want of
   proper sustenance. Cf. Jonson, *Cynthia's Revels*, II.v.18ff.: 'all the ladies and gallants lie languishing upon the rushes ... and without we return quickly, they are
   all, as a youth would say, no better than a few trouts cast ashore, or a dish of eels
   in a sandbag'.
141 *ballets* ballads commemorating the deceased
142 *brokers* pawnbrokers or jobbers, but also pimps
143 *wardropes* a variant form of 'wardrobe'; but *OED* gives independently 'a rope for
   some mechanical purpose', and the intended quibble is evident

MARY
No poison, sir, but serves us for some use,
Which is confirmed in her.
SEBASTIAN   Peace, peace.
Foot, I did hear him sure, where'er he be.
MOLL
Who did you hear?
SEBASTIAN   My father.
'Twas like a sight of his, I must be wary.   150
SIR ALEXANDER
No, wilt not be. Am I alone so wretched
That nothing takes? I'll put him to his plunge for't.
SEBASTIAN
Life, here he comes. – Sir, I beseech you take it,
Your way of teaching does so much content me,
I'll make it four pound, here's forty shillings, sir: 155
I think I name it right (help me, good Moll),
Forty in hand.
MOLL   Sir, you shall pardon me,
I have more of the meanest scholar I can teach,
This pays me more than you have offered yet.
SEBASTIAN
At the next quarter   160
When I receive the means my father 'lows me,
You shall have t'other forty.
SIR ALEXANDER   This were well now,
Were't to a man whose sorrows had blind eyes,
But mine behold his follies and untruths
With two clear glasses. – How now?   [Comes forward]
SEBASTIAN   Sir.
SIR ALEXANDER   What's he there?   165
SEBASTIAN
You're come in good time, sir, I've a suit to you,
I'd crave your present kindness.
SIR ALEXANDER   What is he there?
SEBASTIAN
A gentleman, a musician, sir, one of excellent fingering.

---

148 *Foot* i.e. 's foot (for 'God's foot')
150 *sight* sigh
152 *to his plunge* into a dilemma
155 *forty shillings* There were twenty shillings to a pound.
159 *This* i.e the meanest scholar
162–3 Cf. *The Honest Whore*, part 1, II.i.277: 'This were well now, to one but newly fledged.'

SIR ALEXANDER
  [*Aside*] Ay, I think so, I wonder how they scaped her.
SEBASTIAN
  Has the most delicate stroke, sir.   170
SIR ALEXANDER
  A stroke indeed, I feel it at my heart.
SEBASTIAN
  Puts down all your famous musicians.
SIR ALEXANDER
  Ay, a whore may put down a hundred of 'em.
SEBASTIAN
  Forty shillings is the agreement, sir, between us:
  Now sir, my present means mounts but to half on't.   175
SIR ALEXANDER
  And he stands upon the whole.
SEBASTIAN   Ay indeed does he, sir.
SIR ALEXANDER
  And will do still, he'll ne'er be in other tale.
SEBASTIAN
  Therefore I'd stop his mouth, sir, and I could.
SIR ALEXANDER
  Hum, true, there is no other way indeed; –
  [*Aside*] His folly hardens, shame must needs succeed.   180
  – Now sir, I understand you profess music.
MOLL
  I am a poor servant to that liberal science, sir.
SIR ALEXANDER
  Where is it you teach?
MOLL   Right against Clifford's Inn.
SIR ALEXANDER
  Hum, that's a fit place for it: you have many scholars?

169 *how they scaped her* i.e. how she, supposed light-fingered, managed not to pick up the jewels etc., laid out to trap her
172 *Puts down* (1) surpasses, (2) overthrows, with a hint of the sexual disease she may give them
174 *Forty shillings is the agreement* This seems not to square with the trick thought up earlier (ll. 155ff.).
177 *And will ... tale* i.e. he'll not be paid: he will always be in that position, there will be no other reckoning
178 *and* chiefly in the sense of 'if', but a play on the other sense is pleasant
183 *Clifford's Inn*, next to the church of St Dunstan in the West, Fleet Street, was the oldest Inn in Chancery: it was the seat of all six attorneys of the Palace Court, and it was said that more misery emanated from this small spot than from any one of the most populous counties in England (*Old and New London*, I, 92).

MOLL
    And some of worth, whom I may call my masters.   185
SIR ALEXANDER
    [*Aside*] Ay true, a company of whoremasters.
    – You teach to sing too?
MOLL   Marry do I sir.
SIR ALEXANDER
    I think you'll find an apt scholar of my son, especially for
    prick-song.
MOLL
    I have much hope of him.   190
SIR ALEXANDER
    [*Aside*] I am sorry for't, I have the less for that. – You can
    play any lesson?
MOLL
    At first sight, sir.
SIR ALEXANDER
    There's a thing called the witch, can you play that?
MOLL
    I would be sorry anyone should mend me in't.   195
SIR ALEXANDER
    [*Aside*] Ay, I believe thee, thou hast so bewitched my son,
    No care will mend the work that thou hast done:
    I have bethought myself, since my art fails,
    I'll make her policy the art to trap her.
    Here are four angels marked with holes in them   200
    Fit for his cracked companions, gold he will give her,
    These will I make induction to her ruin,
    And rid shame from my house, grief from my heart.
    – Here, son, in what you take content and pleasure,
    Want shall not curb you; pay the gentleman   205
    His latter half in gold.
SEBASTIAN   I thank you, sir.

---

187 *You teach to sing too* i.e. in the low sense, to copulate (see Eric Partridge,
    Shakespeare's Bawdy (1956), p. 187). Cf. *A Chaste Maid*, II.i.52, and *Troilus and
    Cressida*, V.ii.9ff.
189 *prick-song* Music sung from notes written or 'pricked', as distinguished from that
    learnt by ear. Sexual quibbles on this word are legion in contemporary plays.
192 *lesson* a musical exercise or composition specially written for teaching
194 *the witch* This seems to have been the name of several popular pieces.
195 *mend* probably in the sense of 'surpass', though 'improve' is possible
200 *angels marked with holes in them* The holes are evidently punched through the
    middle (see V.ii.241). The trick seems to be to land Moll either with spoiled
    coins, the possession of which would be an offence, or with marked ones which
    could later be sworn to be stolen. Angels were at this time worth 10 shillings.

SIR ALEXANDER
  [*Aside*] Oh may the operation on't end three:
  In her, life; shame in him; and grief in me.   *Exit*
SEBASTIAN
  Faith thou shalt have 'em, 'tis my father's gift,
  Never was man beguiled with better shift.   210
MOLL
  He that can take me for a male musician,
  I cannot choose but make him my instrument
  And play upon him.   *Exeunt omnes*

[Act IV, Scene ii]

Enter MISTRESS GALLIPOT *and* MISTRESS OPENWORK

MISTRESS GALLIPOT
  Is then that bird of yours, Master Goshawk, so wild?
MISTRESS OPENWORK
  A goshawk, a puttock; all for prey: he angles for fish, but
  he loves flesh better.
MISTRESS GALLIPOT
  Is't possible his smooth face should have wrinkles in't, and
  we not see them?   5
MISTRESS OPENWORK
  Possible? Why, have not many handsome legs in silk stock-
  ings villainous splay feet for all their great roses?
MISTRESS GALLIPOT
  Troth sirrah, thou sayst true.

212–13 *make him my instrument And play upon him* another reminiscence of *Hamlet*
  (cf. III.ii.364f.)

  2 *puttock* kite or buzzard, but applied generally to birds of prey. Goshawks (which
    were once commoner in England than now) are not fish-eaters, but could well
    have been confused with ospreys or even, by such as Mistress Openwork, with
    herons. 'Fish' has long been cant for loose women or female genitals.
  4 *his smooth face* Cf. Dekker's *Seven Deadly Sins of London* (1606), V, 36: 'They
    knew how smooth soever his looks were, there was a devil in his bosom.'
  6–7 *silk stockings* Stubbes and other puritans were particularly severe on the ex-
    travagance of silk stockings 'curiously knit with open seam down the leg, with
    quirks and clocks about the ankles, and sometime (haply) interlaced with gold
    or silver threads ... The time hath been, when one might have clothed all his
    body well, from top to toe, for less than a pair of these nether stocks will cost'
    (*Anatomy of Abuses*, p. 31).
  7 *roses* knots of ribbons worn on the shoe (still, or again, fashionable in Jane
    Austen's time): see the illustration on the title-page

MISTRESS OPENWORK
Didst never see an archer, as thou'st walked by Bunhill,
look a-squint when he drew his bow? 10
MISTRESS GALLIPOT
Yes, when his arrows have fline toward Islington, his eyes
have shot clean contrary towards Pimlico.
MISTRESS OPENWORK
For all the world, so does Master Goshawk double with
me.
MISTRESS GALLIPOT
Oh fie upon him, if he double once he's not for me. 15
MISTRESS OPENWORK
Because Goshawk goes in a shag-ruff band, with a face
sticking up in't which shows like an agate set in a cramp-
ring, he thinks I'm in love with him.
MISTRESS GALLIPOT
'Las, I think he takes his mark amiss in thee.
MISTRESS OPENWORK
He has by often beating into me made me believe that my 20
husband kept a whore.
MISTRESS GALLIPOT
Very good.
MISTRESS OPENWORK
Swore to me that my husband this very morning went in a
boat with a tilt over it, to the Three Pigeons at Brainford,
and his punk with him under his tilt. 25

---

9 *thou'st* ed. (tho'ast Q)
  Bunhill The old artillery ground, next to the famous cemetery, just west of the
  site of Finsbury Square, was regularly used for archery matches. Bullen quotes
  from the *Remembrancia* that, in September 1623, Middleton received 20 marks
  'for his services at the shooting on Bunhill, and at the Conduit Head before the
  Lord Mayor and Aldermen'.
11 *fline* flown.
12 *Pimlico* not the familiar one near Victoria, but a part of Hoxton between New
  North Road and Hoxton Street. It was much frequented 'for the sake of the fresh
  air and the cakes and ale for which it was famous' (Sugden). Cf. Jonson, *The
  Alchemist*, V.ii.17ff.: 'Gallants, men, and women, / And of all sorts, tag-rag, been
  seen to flock here / In threaves, these ten weeks, as to a second Hogsden, / In
  days of Pimlico.' There are many contemporary references. The name may originally have been that of the owner of an alehouse.
13 *double* use duplicity, act deceitfully
17–18 *an agate set in a cramp-ring* Cramp-rings were worn on the finger as a
  protection against cramp and falling-sickness: in pre-Reformation times they
  were hallowed each Good Friday by the king or queen. For the slang use, see
  V.i.210 n.
24 *tilt* an awning over a boat   25 *punk* whore

MISTRESS GALLIPOT
That were wholesome.

MISTRESS OPENWORK
I believed it, fell a-swearing at him, cursing of harlots,
made me ready to hoise up sail and be there as soon as he.

MISTRESS GALLIPOT
So, so.

MISTRESS OPENWORK
And for that voyage Goshawk comes hither incontinently: 30
but sirrah, this water-spaniel dives after no duck but me,
his hope is having me at Brainford to make me cry quack.

MISTRESS GALLIPOT
Art sure of it?

MISTRESS OPENWORK
Sure of it? My poor innocent Openwork came in as I was
poking my ruff, presently hit I him i'the teeth with the   35
Three Pigeons: he forswore all, I up and opened all, and
now stands he in a shop hard by, like a musket on a rest,
to hit Goshawk i'the eye, when he comes to fetch me to the
boat.

MISTRESS GALLIPOT
Such another lame gelding offered to carry me through   40
thick and thin – Laxton, sirrah – but I am rid of him now.

MISTRESS OPENWORK
Happy is the woman can be rid of 'em all; 'las, what are
your whisking gallants to our husbands, weigh 'em rightly
man for man?

MISTRESS GALLIPOT
Troth, mere shallow things.   45

MISTRESS OPENWORK
Idle simple things, running heads, and yet let 'em run over
us never so fast, we shopkeepers, when all's done, are sure

---

30 *incontinently* straightaway, punning on the sense of unable to resist sexual ap-
petite
35 *poking my ruff* crimping the folds of the ruff with a poking-stick, a rod made of
horn, bone, or latterly of steel so that it could be applied hot
37 *like a musket on a rest* The old matchlock musket was very heavy and needed a rest
to support the barrel to ensure accuracy of aim; it consisted of a wooden pole with
an iron fork at the upper end to rest the musket in, and a spike at the bottom to
fix it in the ground. The soldier carried it by a lanyard over his shoulder.
43 *whisking* smart or lively
46 *running* flighty, perhaps with a secondary sense of fluent or plausible

to have 'em in our purse-nets at length, and when they are
in, Lord, what simple animals they are.

[MISTRESS GALLIPOT   ]   50

MISTRESS OPENWORK
    Then they hang the head.
MISTRESS GALLIPOT
    Then they droop.
MISTRESS OPENWORK
    Then they write letters.
MISTRESS GALLIPOT
    Then they cog.
MISTRESS OPENWORK
    Then deal they underhand with us, and we must ingle with   55
    our husbands abed, and we must swear they are our
    cousins, and able to do us a pleasure at court.
MISTRESS GALLIPOT
    And yet when we have done our best, all's but put into a
    riven dish, we are but frumped at and libelled upon.

48 *purse-nets* Bag-shaped nets of which the mouth could be drawn together with a
    string: they were used especially for catching rabbits. 'Rabbit' or 'coney' was also
    thieves' cant for a dupe and the purse-net a device by which he was caught (see
    Greene's *Notable Discovery of Cozenage* (1591) in A. V. Judges, *The Elizabethan
    Underworld* (1930), p. 136). Cf. also *The Gull's Horn-Book*, I: 'a rich man's son
    shall no sooner be out of the shell of his minority but he shall straightways be
    ... ta'en in his own purse-nets by fencers and coney-catchers'.
50 Something is at fault in Q here, for Mistress Openwork is given two consecutive
    speeches. The second, 'Then they hang the head', is at the top of a page, and
    the catchword on the previous page is, accordingly, the speech heading. I agree
    with George R. Price ('The Manuscript and Quarto of *The Roaring Girl*', *The
    Library*, fifth series, 11 (1956), 182–3) in thinking that some short speech by
    Mistress Gallipot – which might give the dialogue a more obvious sequence at
    this point – has accidentally been omitted, though at what stage cannot be as-
    certained. Three copies of Q have been reset at this point (see Bowers, pp.
    106–7) and read, among other accidentals, 'Then they hang head' (l. 49) and
    'Then they deal' (l. 53). Perhaps someone spotted the inconsequence of the un-
    corrected text, found after all that it couldn't be easily corrected, but in unlock-
    ing the forme allowed the type to loosen and pie, and reset it carelessly: the 'cor-
    rected' phrases have no authority.
51–2 *Then they hang the head. Then they droop* The sexual innuendoes in this pass-
    age are made plain here: even now the intentions of the two ladies cannot b/
    taken at face value.
54 *cog* fawn, wheedle
55 *ingle* coax, cajole
56–7 *swear they are our cousins* Such a trick is performed on Candido in *The Hon
    Whore*, part 2.
59 *riven* split (the dish of the image would be a wooden trencher)
    frumped at mocked, insulted, browbeaten

MISTRESS OPENWORK
Oh if it were the good Lord's will, there were a law made   60
no citizen should trust any of 'em all.

Enter GOSHAWK

MISTRESS GALLIPOT
Hush sirrah, Goshawk flutters.
GOSHAWK
How now, are you ready?
MISTRESS OPENWORK
Nay are you ready? A little thing you see makes us ready.
GOSHAWK
Us? Why, must she make one i'the voyage?   65
MISTRESS OPENWORK
Oh by any means: do I know how my husband will handle
me?
GOSHAWK
[*Aside*] Foot, how shall I find water to keep these two
mills going? – Well, since you'll needs be clapped under
hatches, if I sail not with you both till all split, hang me up   70
at the mainyard and duck me. – It's but liquoring them
both soundly, and then you shall see their cork heels fly up
high, like two swans when their tails are above water, and
their long necks under water, diving to catch gudgeons. –
Come, come, oars stand ready, the tide's with us, on with   75
those false faces; blow winds and thou shalt take thy husband casting out his net to catch fresh salmon at Brainford.
MISTRESS GALLIPOT
I believe you'll eat of a cod's head of your own dressing
before you reach half way thither.

[*They mask themselves*]

69–70 *clapped under hatches* kept down or in silence; but 'clap' was used catachresti-
cally for 'clip' (= embrace)
70 *till all split* till all suffer shipwreck, or go to pieces: originally, as here, a sailors'
phrase, though soon made over into common use. Cf. *A Midsummer Night's
Dream*, I.ii.32, and *A Chaste Maid*, IV.ii.95.
72 *cork heels* Chopines had cork soles and high cork heels; they were worn outdoors
as a fashionable alternative to clogs.
74 *gudgeons* doubtless with a play on the sense of (easily caught) simpletons (cf. *A
Chaste Maid*, IV.ii.53)
76 *false faces* masks
78 *you'll eat of a cod's head of your own dressing* you'll make a fool of yourself, caught
in your own net: a cod's head is a stupid fellow, but Mistress Gallipot must want
him to be tricked into picking up the sexual suggestion

GOSHAWK
    So, so, follow close, pin as you go.   80

                    Enter LAXTON *muffled*

LAXTON
    Do you hear?
MISTRESS GALLIPOT
    Yes, I thank my ears.
LAXTON
    I must have a bout with your pothecaryship.
MISTRESS GALLIPOT
    At what weapon?
LAXTON
    I must speak with you.   85
MISTRESS GALLIPOT
    No.
LAXTON
    No? You shall.
MISTRESS GALLIPOT
    Shall? Away, soused sturgeon, half fish, half flesh.
LAXTON
    'Faith, gib, are you spitting? I'll cut your tail, puss-cat, for
    this.   90
MISTRESS GALLIPOT
    'Las poor Laxton, I think thy tail's cut already: you're
    worsed.
LAXTON
    If I do not –   *Exit*
GOSHAWK
    Come, ha' you done?

                    Enter MASTER OPENWORK

                'Sfoot Rosamond, your husband.
MASTER OPENWORK
    How now? Sweet Master Goshawk, none more welcome,   95
    I have wanted your embracements: when friends meet,

---

80 *pin* fasten
83 *bout* would normally imply a sexual encounter, but we know this is not Laxton's
    way with Mistress Gallipot.
89 *gib* cat, hence a term of reproach for a scold
91–2 *you're worsed* ed. (your worst Q). You're blemished or worsted. The Q read-
    ing could be understood as an abbreviated challenge – 'do your worst' – but
    'worst' is a regular form of the past participle of the old verb 'to worse', and this
    seems to fit best with the remainder of the line.
96 *wanted your embracements* missed your company

The music of the spheres sounds not more sweet
Than does their conference; who is this? Rosamond?
Wife? How now, sister?
GOSHAWK   Silence if you love me.
MASTER OPENWORK
  Why masked?
MISTRESS OPENWORK Does a mask grieve you, sir?
MASTER OPENWORK   It does.   100
MISTRESS OPENWORK
  Then y'are best get you a-mumming.
GOSHAWK   'Sfoot, you'll spoil all.
MISTRESS GALLIPOT
  May not we cover our bare faces with masks
  As well as you cover your bald heads with hats?
MASTER OPENWORK
  No masks; why, th'are thieves to beauty, that rob eyes
  Of admiration in which true love lies.   105
  Why are masks worn? Why good? Or why desired?
  Unless by their gay covers wits are fired
  To read the vildest looks; many bad faces
  (Because rich gems are treasured up in cases)
  Pass by their privilege current: but as caves   110
  Dam misers' gold, so masks are beauty's graves;
  Men ne'er meet women with such muffled eyes,
  But they curse her that first did masks devise,
  And swear it was some beldam. Come, off with't.

97 *music of the spheres* the music the heavenly bodies were believed to make as they
   moved. The congruity between the ratios of their orbits with musical intervals
   confirmed a concept of divine harmony.
101 *get you a-mumming* The phrase 'to go a-mumming' means to disguise oneself, especially for a mumming play, which was acted with masks in dumb-show: perhaps, therefore, 'you'd best keep silence'. (To play or keep mum meant, as now,
   to be silent.)
110 *Pass by their privilege current* i.e. are received as genuine or honest, because of the
   privilege conferred by masks. Masks were widely used by prostitutes to spread
   their business, but they did not always enable them to pass current: see
   Northward Ho!, I.ii.83: 'we [whores] are not current till we pass from one man
   to another'; and *The Honest Whore*, part 2, IV.i.397f.: 'She (crowned with
   reverend praises) passed by them, I (though with face masked) could not scape
   the hem.'
111 *Dam* The Q reading is 'dambe', which *OED* records only as an erroneous form
   of 'dam', though 'damb' is found for 'damn'. Doubtless there is a *double enten-*
   dre, but the primary sense seems best served by 'dam': misers' gold is blocked
   up, obscured, in caves.
114 *beldam* witch

MISTRESS OPENWORK
 I will not.   115
MASTER OPENWORK
 Good faces masked are jewels kept by sprites:
 Hide none but bad ones, for they poison men's sights,
 Show them as shopkeepers do their broidered stuff,
 By owl-light; fine wares cannot be open enough:
 Prithee, sweet Rose, come strike this sail.
MISTRESS OPENWORK   Sail?
MASTER OPENWORK   Ha!   120
 Yes, wife, strike sail, for storms are in thine eyes.
MISTRESS OPENWORK
 Th'are here, sir, in my brows if any rise.
MASTER OPENWORK
 Ha, brows? What says she, friend? Pray tell me why
 Your two flags were advanced; the comedy,
 Come, what's the comedy?
MISTRESS GALLIPOT   *Westward Ho.*
MASTER OPENWORK   How?   125
MISTRESS OPENWORK
 'Tis *Westward Ho* she says.
GOSHAWK   Are you both mad?
MISTRESS OPENWORK
 Is't market day at Brainford, and your ware
 Not sent up yet?
MASTER OPENWORK What market day? What ware?
MISTRESS OPENWORK
 A pie with three pigeons in't, 'tis drawn and stays your cut-
 ting up.   130

116 *sprites* ed. (spirits Q), i.e. evil spirits
118 *them* ed. (then Q): bad faces ought only to be shown by owl-light when, like the
 inferior quality of shopkeepers' embroidery, they can't be clearly seen
 broidered stuff ordinary coarse fabric made fancy
122 *in my brows* perhaps a remote allusion to a female cuckold's (or cuckquean's)
 horns
124 *Your two flags* Flags with individual symbols were hoisted on the tops of theatres
 an hour or two before a play was due to begin; there is presumably also a play
 on the flag that a boat might carry, and possibly on the slang meaning of apron.
125 *Westward Ho* by Dekker and Webster (1604–5). 'Westward ho!' was the cry of
 watermen going west, as for example towards Brentford from London; cf.
 Twelfth Night, III.i.134.
125 sp MISTRESS GALLIPOT ed. (Mist. Open. Q)
129–30 *stays your cutting up* Cf. III.ii.228 and n.

GOSHAWK
   As you regard my credit -
MASTER OPENWORK
   Art mad?
MISTRESS OPENWORK
   Yes, lecherous goat; baboon.
MASTER OPENWORK
   Baboon? Then toss me in a blanket.
MISTRESS OPENWORK
   Do I it well?   135
MISTRESS GALLIPOT
   Rarely.
GOSHAWK
   Belike, sir, she's not well; best leave her.
MASTER OPENWORK   No,
   I'll stand the storm now how fierce so e'er it blow.
MISTRESS OPENWORK
   Did I for this lose all my friends? Refuse
   Rich hopes and golden fortunes, to be made   140
   A stale to a common whore?
MASTER OPENWORK   This does amaze me.
MISTRESS OPENWORK
   Oh God, oh God, feed at reversion now?
   A strumpet's leaving?
MASTER OPENWORK   Rosamond.
GOSHAWK
   I sweat, would I lay in Cold Harbour.
MISTRESS OPENWORK
   Thou hast struck ten thousand daggers through my heart.   145

133 *baboon* a generalised term of abuse
134 *toss me in a blanket* Tossing in a blanket was a 'rough, irregular form of punish-
    ment' (*OED*), the offender being thrown repeatedly in the air from a blanket
    held slackly from the corners. There is probably a play on blanket-love, mean-
    ing illicit amours.
141 *stale* a mistress turned to ridicule for the amusement of a rival; but the whole
    phrase telescopes this with the sense of 'common stale', a prostitute used by
    thieves as a decoy
142 *at reversion* (in legal terms) in succession, conditionally on the expiry of a grant
    or at death; but reversions are also the left-overs of a dish or meal
144 *Cold Harbour* The name of a former mansion in Upper Thames Street, which
    passed through the hands of a remarkable number of noble owners and was re-
    placed in the mid-sixteenth century by a collection of tenements which quickly
    became a haunt of poverty and an ad-hoc sanctuary for those wanting to disap-
    pear, as undoubtedly Goshawk wants at this moment (the alternative spelling
    'Cole' can mean a cheat); but he is of course playing on the literal meaning of
    the name.

MASTER OPENWORK
Not I, by heaven, sweet wife.
MISTRESS OPENWORK   Go, devil, go;
That which thou swear'st by damns thee.
GOSHAWK
'S heart, will you undo me?
MISTRESS OPENWORK
Why stay you here? The star by which you sail
Shines yonder above Chelsea; you lose your shore;   150
If this moon light you, seek out your light whore.
MASTER OPENWORK
Ha?
MISTRESS OPENWORK Push, your western pug –
GOSHAWK   Zounds, now hell roars.
MISTRESS OPENWORK
With whom you tilted in a pair of oars,
This very morning.
MASTER OPENWORK   Oars?
MISTRESS OPENWORK   At Brainford, sir.
MASTER OPENWORK
Rack not my patience: Master Goshawk,   155
Some slave has buzzed this into her, has he not?
I run a tilt in Brainford with a woman?
'Tis a lie:
What old bawd tells thee this? 'Sdeath, 'tis a lie.
MISTRESS OPENWORK
'Tis one to thy face shall justify all that I speak.   160
MASTER OPENWORK
Ud'soul, do but name that rascal.

149ff. For thirty lines (149–80) Q prints a medley of verse and prose: the rhymes,
    some evident pentameters, an occasional median capital, and the fact that some
    is printed as verse suggest that it should all be, though the result is undoubt-
    edly rough.
149–51 *The star ... whore* Punctuation ed. (star, ... sail, ... Chelsea; ... light you:
    ... whore. Q) I take it that this means 'you are missing your landing by not at-
    tending to the star in the west; if that's the way you want to go, now is the time'.
152 sp MISTRESS OPENWORK ed. (Mist. Gal. Q)
    western pug (png Q) a pug is a harlot, but western pugs were bargees who navi-
    gated down the Thames to London, as from Brentford among other places
154 *tilted* jousted, but also (of a boat) pitched in the waves; and cf. above l. 24 and
    n., and *1 Henry IV*, II.iii.92, 'to tilt with lips'
157 *run a tilt* (or run a-tilt) engage in a tilt or joust
160 *'Tis one to thy face* (*stet* Q). Bullen suggests ' 'Tis one who to thy face...'
161 *Ud'soul* God's soul.

MISTRESS OPENWORK
    No sir, I will not.
GOSHAWK   Keep thee there, girl: – then!
MASTER OPENWORK
    Sister, know you this varlet?
MISTRESS GALLIPOT   Yes.
MASTER OPENWORK   Swear true.
    Is there a rogue so low damned? A second Judas?
    A common hangman? Cutting a man's throat?   165
    Does it to his face? Bite me behind my back?
    A cur dog? Swear if you know this hell-hound.
MISTRESS GALLIPOT
    In truth I do.
MASTER OPENWORK
            His name?
MISTRESS GALLIPOT   Not for the world,
    To have you to stab him.
GOSHAWK   Oh brave girls, worth gold.
MASTER OPENWORK
    A word, honest Master Goshawk.

                Draw[s] out his sword

GOSHAWK   What do you mean, sir?   170
MASTER OPENWORK
    Keep off, and if the devil can give a name
    To this new fury, holla it through my ear,
    Or wrap it up in some hid character:
    I'll ride to Oxford and watch out mine eyes
    But I'll hear the brazen head speak: or else   175
    Show me but one hair of his head or beard,
    That I may sample it; if the fiend I meet
    In mine own house, I'll kill him: – the street,
    Or at the church door: – there ('cause he seeks to untie
    The knot God fastens) he deserves most to die.   180

163 sp MASTER OPENWORK ed. (Mis. Open. Q)
169 *worth gold* Proverbial: cf. Munday, *Fedele and Fortunio* (1585), l. 1703: 'such a
    girl is worth gold in a dear year'; and the subtitle of Heywood's *Fair Maid of the
    West* – 'A girl worth gold'.
173 *hid character* code
174–7 *I'll ride to Oxford* ... Friar Bacon and Friar Bungay spent seven years making
    a brass head, so that they could ask it whether it were possible to build a wall of
    brass round Britain. Unfortunately they neglected to note the time at which the
    head was to speak and so received no distinct answer. Cf. *The Famous Historie of
    Fryer Bacon* and Greene's *Honourable History of Friar Bacon and Friar Bungay* (to
    which Middleton had in 1602 written a prologue and epilogue), esp. sc. xi.

MISTRESS OPENWORK
  My husband titles him.
MASTER OPENWORK   Master Goshawk, pray sir,
  Swear to me that you know him or know him not,
  Who makes me at Brainford to take up a petticoat
  Besides my wife's.
GOSHAWK   By heaven that man I know not.
MISTRESS OPENWORK
  Come, come, you lie.
GOSHAWK   Will you not have all out?   185
  By heaven, I know no man beneath the moon
  Should do you wrong, but if I had his name,
  I'd print it in text letters.
MISTRESS OPENWORK   Print thine own then,
  Didst not thou swear to me he kept his whore?
MISTRESS GALLIPOT
  And that in sinful Brainford they would commit   190
  That which our lips did water at, sir, – ha?
MISTRESS OPENWORK
  Thou spider, that hast woven thy cunning web
  In mine own house t'insnare me: hast not thou
  Sucked nourishment even underneath this roof,
  And turned it all to poison, spitting it   195
  On thy friend's face (my husband), he as 'twere sleeping?
  Only to leave him ugly to mine eyes,
  That they might glance on thee?
MISTRESS GALLIPOT   Speak, are these lies?
GOSHAWK
  Mine own shame me confounds.
MASTER OPENWORK   No more, he's stung;
  Who'd think that in one body there could dwell   200
  Deformity and beauty, heaven and hell?
  Goodness I see is but outside: we all set,
  In rings of gold, stones that be counterfeit:
  I thought you none.

---

188 *text letters* large or capital letters in handwriting
191 *our lips did water at* Cf. III.ii.21.
195 *turned it all to poison* Spiders were commonly supposed to be poisonous, though,
    according to one view, only if known to be there. Cf. *The Winter's Tale*, II.i.40,
    and *No Wit, No Help, like a Woman's*, II.i.392–3.
199 sp MASTER OPENWORK ed. (Mist. Open. Q)
203 *counterfeit* Q has the spelling 'counterfet', which gives a perfect rhyme.

GOSHAWK   Pardon me.
MASTER OPENWORK   Truth I do.
  This blemish grows in nature, not in you,   205
  For man's creation stick even moles in scorn
  On fairest cheeks: wife, nothing is perfect born.
MISTRESS OPENWORK
  I thought you had been born perfect.
MASTER OPENWORK
  What's this whole world but a gilt rotten pill?
  For at the heart lies the old chore still.   210
  I'll tell you, Master Goshawk, – Ay, in your eye
  I have seen wanton fire, and then to try
  The soundness of my judgment, I told you
  I kept a whore, made you believe 'twas true,
  Only to feel how your pulse beat, but find   215
  The world can hardly yield a perfect friend.
  Come, come, a trick of youth, and 'tis forgiven.
  This rub put by, our love shall run more even.
MISTRESS OPENWORK
  You'll deal upon men's wives no more?
GOSHAWK   No: you teach me
  A trick for that.
MISTRESS OPENWORK Troth do not, they'll o'erreach thee.   220
MASTER OPENWORK
  Make my house yours, sir, still.
GOSHAWK   No.
MASTER OPENWORK   I say you shall:
  Seeing, thus besieged, it holds out, 'twill never fall.

         Enter MASTER GALLIPOT, *and* GREENWIT *like a sumner,*
                  LAXTON *muffled aloof off*

OMNES
  How now?
MASTER GALLIPOT
  With me, sir?

210 *chore* i.e. core, alluding here to Adam's apple
211 *Ay* ed. (E.C.) I Q (*in* Gomme)
218 *rub* impediment: the image in the rest of the line suggests the physical rubs or
    roughnesses in a bowling alley, by which the bowls were deflected from their true
    course. Cf. III.ii.171–2 and n.
219 *deal upon* set to work on, but to deal with a woman also means to have sexual in-
    tercourse with her
220 *A trick for that* perhaps as in the proverbial phrase 'a trick worth two of that'.
    (But cf. *A Trick to Catch the Old One*, IV.iv.208.)
222 sd 1 *sumner* an official employed to summon persons to appear in court

GREENWIT

You, sir. I have gone snaffling up and down by your door   225
this hour to watch for you.

MISTRESS GALLIPOT

What's the matter, husband?

GREENWIT

I have caught a cold in my head, sir, by sitting up late in
the Rose tavern, but I hope you understand my speech.

MASTER GALLIPOT

So sir.   230

GREENWIT

I cite you by the name of Hippocrates Gallipot, and you by
the name of Prudence Gallipot, to appear upon Crastino,
do you see, Crastino sancti Dunstani, this Easter term, in
Bow Church.

MASTER GALLIPOT

Where, sir? What says he?   235

GREENWIT

Bow: Bow Church, to answer to a libel of precontract on
the part and behalf of the said Prudence and another: y'are
best, sir, take a copy of the citation; 'tis but twelvepence.

OMNES

A citation?

MASTER GALLIPOT

You pocky-nosed rascal, what slave fees you to this?   240

LAXTON

Slave? I ha' nothing to do with you, do you hear, sir?

---

225 *snaffling* OED gives 'saunter' virtually on the strength of this line alone. But, as
      the reference to his cold three lines later shows, the word is simply a variant form
      of 'snuffling' – and one which is well represented in OED.
229 *Rose* a fairly common name for inns and taverns: one stood on Holborn Hill,
      from which coaches departed for Brentford; Greenwit's may rather have been
      that near Temple Bar, frequented by lawyers
231 *Hippocrates* The name of the great Greek physician would be a suitable, if
      grandiose, one for an apothecary.
233 *Crastino sancti Dunstani* on the morrow of St Dunstan (i.e. 19 May)
236 *Bow Church* The famous church on the south side of Cheapside near the corner
      of Bread Street was formerly the seat of the Court of Arches, which, according
      to one tradition, was (like the church – St Mary-le-Bow or St Mary de Arcubus)
      named after the arched buttresses or bows which have always held up the
      steeple. But it may have sat in the early medieval crypt, the massive arches of
      which alone survived the Great Fire and were incorporated into Wren's rebuild-
      ing. (The crypt survived the blitz of 1940–4 also.) To this court came all appeals
      in ecclesiastical matters within the province of Canterbury.
      libel in ecclesiastical law, the plaintiff's written declaration of charges in a cause

GOSHAWK

    Laxton, is't not? – what vagary is this?

MASTER GALLIPOT

    Trust me, I thought, sir, this storm long ago

    Had been full laid, when (if you be remembered)

    I paid you the last fifteen pound, besides   245

    The thirty you had first; for then you swore –

LAXTON

    Tush, tush sir, oaths;

    Truth, yet I'm loath to vex you, – tell you what:

    Make up the money I had a hundred pound,

    And take your bellyful of her.

MASTER GALLIPOT   A hundred pound?   250

MISTRESS GALLIPOT

    What, a hundred pound? He gets none: what, a hundred

        pound?

MASTER GALLIPOT

    Sweet Pru, be calm, the gentleman offers thus,

    If I will make the moneys that are past

    A hundred pound, he will discharge all courts,

    And give his bond never to vex us more.   255

MISTRESS GALLIPOT

    A hundred pound? 'Las, take, sir, but threescore,

    Do you seek my undoing?

LAXTON   I'll not bate one sixpence, –

    I'll maul you, puss, for spitting.

MISTRESS GALLIPOT   Do thy worst, –

    Will fourscore stop thy mouth?

LAXTON   No.

MISTRESS GALLIPOT   Y'are a slave,

    Thou cheat, I'll now tear money from thy throat: 260

    Husband, lay hold on yonder tawny-coat.

GREENWIT

    Nay, gentlemen, seeing your women are so hot, I must

    lose my hair in their company, I see.

                 [*Takes off his wig*]

---

261 *tawny-coat* Ecclesiastical apparitors (servants of the court) wore tawny-coloured
    livery. Greenwit is so disguised.

263 *lose my hair* alluding to the most frequent and obvious effect of syphilis. Q has
    'loose', and the two words were indeed often not clearly distinguished: a light
    pun is possible.

MISTRESS OPENWORK
His hair sheds off, and yet he speaks not so much in the
nose as he did before.   265
GOSHAWK
He has had the better chirurgeon. – Master Greenwit, is
your wit so raw as to play no better a part than a sumner's?
MASTER GALLIPOT
I pray, who plays a knack to know an honest man in this
company?
MISTRESS GALLIPOT
Dear husband, pardon me, I did dissemble,   270
Told thee I was his precontracted wife,
When letters came from him for thirty pound,
I had no shift but that.
MASTER GALLIPOT   A very clean shift:
But able to make me lousy. On.
MISTRESS GALLIPOT   Husband, I plucked –
When he had tempted me to think well of him –   275
Got feathers from thy wings, to make him fly
More lofty.
MASTER GALLIPOT
A' the top of you, wife: on.
MISTRESS GALLIPOT
He having wasted them, comes now for more,
Using me as a ruffian doth his whore,
Whose sin keeps him in breath: by heaven I vow   280
Thy bed he never wronged, more than he does now.
MASTER GALLIPOT
My bed? Ha, ha, like enough, a shop-board will serve
To have a cuckold's coat cut out upon:
Of that we'll talk hereafter – y'are a villain.
LAXTON
Hear me but speak, sir, you shall find me none.   285

264–5 *in the nose* Cf. above, l. 228; another effect of syphilis is to make the nose
    swollen and pustular.
267 *no better a part than a sumner's* Greene in his *Notable Discovery of Cozenage* gives
    instances of coney-catchers learning a smattering of law and going dressed as
    sumners or apparitors.
268 *A Knack to Know an Honest Man* is the title of an early anonymous comedy; and
    the phrase and its complement, 'a knack to know a knave', were in common
    proverbial use.
273–4 lineation ed. (*prose* Q)
273 *shift* Gallipot's answer plays on the sense of petticoat.
276 *Got* ed. (E.C.) (Get Q) Gomme and Mulholland give *Gelt*. In my reading
    'plucked' is intransitive and its meaning is reiterated in 'Got feathers'.

OMNES
> Pray sir, be patient and hear him.

MASTER GALLIPOT
> I am muzzled for biting, sir, use me how you will.

LAXTON
> The first hour that your wife was in my eye,
> Myself with other gentlemen sitting by
> In your shop tasting smoke, and speech being used   290
> That men who have fairest wives are most abused
> And hardly scaped the horn, your wife maintained
> That only such spots in city dames were stained
> Justly but by men's slanders: for her own part,
> She vowed that you had so much of her heart,   295
> No man by all his wit, by any wile
> Never so fine spun, should yourself beguile
> Of what in her was yours.

MASTER GALLIPOT   Yet, Pru, 'tis well:
> Play out your game at Irish, sir: who wins?

MISTRESS OPENWORK
> The trial is when she comes to bearing.   300

LAXTON
> I scorned one woman thus should brave all men,
> And (which more vexed me) a she-citizen.
> Therefore I laid siege to her, out she held,
> Gave many a brave repulse, and me compelled
> With shame to sound retreat to my hot lust;   305
> Then seeing all base desires raked up in dust,
> And that to tempt her modest ears I swore
> Ne'er to presume again, she said her eye
> Would ever give me welcome honestly,
> And, since I was a gentleman, if it run low,   310
> She would my state relieve, not to o'erthrow
> Your own and hers: did so; then seeing I wrought
> Upon her meekness, me she set at nought;
> And yet to try if I could turn that tide,
> You see what stream I strove with, but, sir, I swear   315
> By heaven, and by those hopes men lay up there,

292–4 *your wife maintained* ... perhaps this means that she maintained that such
stains on city dames came in truth only by slanders (cf. III.i.84ff.)

292 *horn* the sign of the cuckold

299 *Irish* a game resembling backgammon (fully described in Cotton's *Compleat
Gamester* of 1674)

300 *when she comes to bearing* To bear at backgammon is to remove a piece at the end
of a game: cf. *Northward Ho!*, IV.i.267: 'she'd win any game when she came to
bearing'. There is, of course, a quibble on bearing a child.

I neither have nor had a base intent
To wrong your bed; what's done is merriment:
Your gold I pay back with this interest,
When I had most power to do't I wronged you least.   320
MASTER GALLIPOT
  If this no gullery be sir –
OMNES   No, no, on my life.
MASTER GALLIPOT
  Then, sir, I am beholden – not to you, wife –
  But Master Laxton, to your want of doing ill,
  Which it seems you have not. Gentlemen,
  Tarry and dine here all.
MASTER OPENWORK   Brother, we have a jest   325
  As good as yours to furnish out a feast.
MASTER GALLIPOT
  We'll crown our table with it: wife, brag no more
  Of holding out: who most brags is most whore.

Exeunt

[Act V, Scene i]

Enter JACK DAPPER, MOLL, SIR BEAUTEOUS GANYMEDE,
and SIR THOMAS LONG

JACK DAPPER
  But prithee Master Captain Jack, be plain and perspicuous
  with me: was it your Meg of Westminster's courage that
  rescued me from the Poultry puttocks indeed?
MOLL
  The valour of my wit, I ensure you, sir, fetched you off
  bravely, when you were i'the forlorn hope among those

319 *this interest* i.e. the substance of the following line
324–5 The invitation to dine is a traditional comic resolution. Cf. the end of
  Bartholomew Fair.

  1 *perspicuous* clear in statement
  2 *Meg of Westminster* The exploits of this Meg (a heroine of somewhat the same
    stamp as the Roaring Girl) are told in *The Life and Pranks of Long Meg of
    Westminster*, 1582. A play about her was acted in 1594–5, and she appears in the
    anti-masque of Jonson's *The Fortunate Isles*; see above p. xix.
  3 *Poultry puttocks* The two kites were presumably attached to the Poultry counter,
    in which Dekker was once imprisoned.
  5 *the forlorn hope* (Dutch *verloren hoop*) was originally a picked body of men
    detached to the front to lead an attack, and hence any group of men in a des-
    perate state

desperates; Sir Beauteous Ganymede here and Sir
Thomas Long heard that cuckoo, my man Trapdoor, sing
the note of your ransom from captivity.

SIR BEAUTEOUS

Uds so, Moll, where's that Trapdoor?

MOLL

Hanged I think by this time; a justice in this town, that   10
speaks nothing but 'Make a mittimus, away with him to
Newgate', used that rogue like a firework to run upon a
line betwixt him and me.

OMNES

How, how?

MOLL

Marry, to lay trains of villainy to blow up my life; I smelt   15
the powder, spied what linstock gave fire to shoot against
the poor captain of the galley-foist, and away slid I my
man like a shovel-board shilling. He struts up and down
the suburbs I think, and eats up whores, feeds upon a
bawd's garbage.   20

SIR THOMAS

Sirrah Jack Dapper.

JACK DAPPER

What sayst, Tom Long?

9 *Uds so* The phrase has no specific meaning: 'Ud' as a form of the name of God
was attached to many other words and syllables in seventeenth-century oaths, as
Udsbud, Udshash, Udzooks. Uds so is probably a transformation, ultimately, of
catso: cf. III.ii.153.

11 *mittimus* (Lat. 'we send') a warrant under the hand of a J.P. ordering the person
named to be kept in custody until delivered to a court of law

12–13 *a firework to run upon a line* The expression, as Bullen notes, is not uncom-
mon. Dyce quotes from *The Whore of Babylon* (III.i.89f.): 'Let us behold these
fireworks that must run / Upon short lines of life.' The line is a train or fuse of
gunpowder (see l. 15) which combusts along its length from one end to the
other.

16 *linstock* a staff, very like a musket rest, which held a gunner's match or lunt

17 *galley-foist* a state barge, especially that of the Lord Mayor of London.
Mulholland notes that 'Dekker seems to have been fond of using the term for
large women.'

18 *shovel-board shilling* Shovel-board, or shuffleboard, a game resembling shove-
halfpenny in which silver pieces were knocked along a very long highly polished
table into compartments marked out at the end, was widely popular. The coins
most commonly used were Edward VI shillings (see *Merry Wives of Windsor*,
I.i.156), specially polished so that they were proverbially slippery. Cf. Jonson,
Every Man in His Humour (English version), III.v.16–17: 'They ... made it run
as smooth off the tongue as a shove-groat shilling.'

SIR THOMAS

Thou hadst a sweet-faced boy, hail-fellow with thee, to
your little Gull: how is he spent?

JACK DAPPER

Troth I whistled the poor little buzzard off o' my fist, be-   25
cause when he waited upon me at the ordinaries, the gallants hit me i'the teeth still, and said I looked like a painted
alderman's tomb, and the boy at my elbow like a death's
head. – Sirrah Jack, Moll.

MOLL

What says my little Dapper?   30

SIR BEAUTEOUS

Come, come, walk and talk, walk and talk.

JACK DAPPER

Moll and I'll be i'the midst.

MOLL

These knights shall have squires' places, belike then: well
Dapper, what say you?

JACK DAPPER

Sirrah Captain Mad Mary, the gull my own father, Dapper   35
Sir Davy, laid these London boot-halers, the catchpolls, in
ambush to set upon me.

OMNES

Your father? Away, Jack.

JACK DAPPER

By the tassels of this handkercher 'tis true, and what was

---

23 *hail-fellow* intimate

25 *whistled ... off* a technical term in falconry, meaning to dismiss by whistling (cf.
  Othello, III.iii.262)

27 *hit me i'the teeth* reproached or mocked me (cf. to throw it in one's teeth): cf. *A
  Fair Quarrel*, II.ii.109

27–8 *a painted alderman's tomb* The Elizabethan and early Stuart period was the
  great time for half-acre tombs, which were showily painted. A death's head is a
  common accompaniment of the effigies.

33 *These knights ... places* Squires, as the knights' armour-bearers, would take their
  positions outside those whom they served.

35–6 *Dapper Sir Davy* ((Dapper) Sir Dauy Q). Perhaps we should read 'Sir Davy
  Dapper', but Jack may be making a joke on his father's name.

36 *boot-halers* freebooters or highwaymen; Dekker uses the word several times
  catchpolls Cf. III.i.39.

39 *handkercher* the customary spoken form of the word, particularly in Midland and
  southern dialect, until the eighteenth century, but common also in literary use
  (cf. *All's Well that Ends Well*, V.iii.321). They were often extravagantly fringed
  and tasselled.

his warlike stratagem, think you? He thought because a   40
wicker cage tames a nightingale, a lousy prison could make
an ass of me.

OMNES
A nasty plot.

JACK DAPPER
Ay: as though a counter, which is a park in which all the
wild beasts of the city run head by head, could tame me.   45

Enter the LORD NOLAND

MOLL
Yonder comes my Lord Noland.

OMNES
Save you, my Lord.

LORD NOLAND
Well met, gentlemen all, good Sir Beauteous Ganymede,
Sir Thomas Long. And how does Master Dapper?

JACK DAPPER
Thanks, my Lord.   50

MOLL
No tobacco, my Lord?

LORD NOLAND
No 'faith, Jack.

JACK DAPPER
My Lord Noland, will you go to Pimlico with us? We are
making a boon voyage to that nappy land of spice-cakes.

LORD NOLAND
Here's such a merry ging, I could find in my heart to sail   55
to the world's end with such company; come, gentlemen,
let's on.

40–2 The analogy between the caged bird and imprisoned man was a common-
place. Cf. *A Trick to Catch the Old One*, IV.iii.48f. and Jonson, 'To the World',
29ff.
44 *counter* Cf. III.iii.74 and n.
53 *Pimlico* Cf. IV.ii.12 and n.
54 *boon voyage* 'bon voyage' (Fr.). The phrase, like others, was commonly angli-
cised.
nappy heady, intoxicated
spice-cakes In Glapthorne's *Lady Mother* of 1635, III.ii (qu. Sugden under
Pimlico), one character reminds another of walking to Pimlico 'to eat plumcakes
and cream'.
55 *ging* company
56 *the world's end* There was more than one tavern of this name then at some considerable distance from London.

JACK DAPPER
Here's most amorous weather, my Lord.
OMNES
Amorous weather?

They walk

JACK DAPPER
Is not amorous a good word?   60

Enter TRAPDOOR *like a poor soldier with a patch o'er one
eye, and* TEARCAT *with him, all tatters*

TRAPDOOR
Shall we set upon the infantry, these troops of foot?
Zounds, yonder comes Moll, my whorish master and mis-
tress; would I had her kidneys between my teeth.
TEARCAT
I had rather have a cow-heel.
TRAPDOOR
Zounds, I am so patched up, she cannot discover me: we'll   65
on.
TEARCAT
Alla corago then.
TRAPDOOR
Good your honours and worships, enlarge the ears of com-
miseration, and let the sound of a hoarse military organ-
pipe penetrate your pitiful bowels to extract out of them so   70
many small drops of silver as may give a hard straw-bed
lodging to a couple of maimed soldiers.
JACK DAPPER
Where are you maimed?
TEARCAT
In both our nether limbs.
MOLL
Come, come, Dapper, let's give 'em something: 'las poor   75
men, what money have you? By my troth I love a soldier
with my soul.
SIR BEAUTEOUS
Stay, stay, where have you served?
SIR THOMAS
In any part of the Low Countries?

64 *cow-heel* the foot of a cow or ox stewed to form a jelly
67 *Alla corago* a corruption of the Italian *coraggio* (courage)

TRAPDOOR

    Not in the Low Countries, if it please your manhood, but   80
in Hungary against the Turk at the siege of Belgrade.

LORD NOLAND

    Who served there with you, sirrah?

TRAPDOOR

    Many Hungarians, Moldavians, Walachians, and Tran-
sylvanians, with some Sclavonians, and retiring home, sir,
the Venetian galleys took us prisoners, yet freed us, and   85
suffered us to beg up and down the country.

JACK DAPPER

    You have ambled all over Italy then?

TRAPDOOR

    Oh sir, from Venice to Roma, Vecchio, Bononia, Ro-
mania, Bolonia, Modena, Piacenza, and Tuscana with all
her cities, as Pistoia, Valteria, Mountepulchena, Arezzo,   90
with the Siennois, and diverse others.

MOLL

    Mere rogues, put spurs to 'em once more.

JACK DAPPER

    Thou look'st like a strange creature, a fat butter-box, yet
speak'st English. – What art thou?

TEARCAT

    Ick, mine Here? Ick bin den ruffling Tearcat, den brave   95

81 *the siege of Belgrade* Belgrade has had numerous sieges, the most famous of
    which, that of 1455–6, raised by the great János Hunyadi, seems to have been
    the last before 1611; from 1521 to 1688 the city remained in the hands of the
    Turks. There was, however, constant warfare in Hungary throughout this time,
    and perhaps Trapdoor has muddled memories of the so-called 'Long War'
    (1593–1606), a confused, and often bitter, partly religious struggle involving, as
    well as the Emperor's native Hungarians and the Turks, all the nationalities
    mentioned in the next speech. (In *A Fair Quarrel*, IV.i.33, we hear of roaring in
    Sclavonian, along with other more obviously Londonian dialects.)
88–91 An amble indeed: Vecchio is presumably Civitavecchia, Bononia and
    Bolonia are one and the same, the modern Bologna, Romania is Romagna,
    Valteria Volterra, Mountepulchena Montepulciano. Moll recognises that this is
    no proper journey but a string of names picked up at hearsay.
93 *butter-box* contemptuous term for a Dutchman
95–9 This piece of bastard Dutch is spelt here exactly as in Q (where it is printed
    in black letter), though the punctuation has been regularised. A 'translation'
    must be a matter partly of guesswork, but it isn't entirely gibberish, though some
    words are hard to identify. (I have supposed that, since Tearcat goes once into
    Spanish, he may also include an attempt at a French word: it looks as if *Beasa*
    may be *baiser*.) 'I, sir? I am the ruffling Tearcat, the brave soldier, I have trav-
    elled through all Holland: the rascal who gave more [than] a kiss and a word. I
    beat him with blows on the head; pulled out thence a hundred thousand devils,
    cheerfully, sir.' To ruffle is to swagger, also to handle a woman with rude famil-
    iarity; for the cant use, see below, l. 146 and Appendix.

Soldado, ick bin dorick all Dutchlant gueresen: der Shellum das
meere ine Beasa ine Woert gaeb. Ick slaag um stroakes on tom
Cop: dastick den hundred touzun Divell halle, frollick mine
Here.

SIR BEAUTEOUS

Here, here, let's be rid of their jobbering.   100

MOLL

Not a cross, Sir Beauteous. You base rogues, I have taken
measure of you better than a tailor can, and I'll fit you as
you, monster with one eye, have fitted me.

TRAPDOOR

Your worship will not abuse a soldier.

MOLL

Soldier? Thou deservest to be hanged up by that tongue   105
which dishonours so noble a profession: soldier, you
skeldering varlet? Hold, stand, there should be a trapdoor
hereabouts.

Pull[s] off his patch

TRAPDOOR

The balls of these glaziers of mine, mine eyes, shall be shot
up and down in any hot piece of service for my invincible   110
mistress.

JACK DAPPER

I did not think there had been such knavery in black
patches as now I see.

100 *jobbering* jabbering
101 *Not a cross* From the fourteenth century at the latest coins were frequently
    stamped with a cross on the reverse side: Sir Beauteous has made to get rid of
    them by offering money.
102 *fit* in the sense of 'provide for', as well as literally
103 *monster with one eye* a reference to Trapdoor's patch. Mulholland also notes that
    in *Women Beware Women* a stage trap-door is referred to as 'a devil with one eye'
    (V.i.9).
107 *skeldering* sponging: the term seems to have been used especially of vagabonds
    begging under the guise of old soldiers: cf. Jonson, *Every Man Out Of His*
    Humour, the Characters (description of Shift): 'A threadbare shark; one that
    never was a soldier, yet lives upon lendings. His profession is skeldering and
    odling.' See *Lanthorn and Candlelight*, p. xxiv, for a description of their methods
    of begging.
109 *glaziers* cant term for eyes
112–13 *black patches* They were worn as ornaments by ladies and fops.

MOLL

Oh sir, he hath been brought up in the Isle of Dogs, and
can both fawn like a spaniel and bite like a mastiff, as he   115
finds occasion.

LORD NOLAND

What are you, sirrah? A bird of this feather too?

TEARCAT

A man beaten from the wars, sir.

SIR THOMAS

I think so, for you never stood to fight.

JACK DAPPER

What's thy name, fellow soldier?   120

TEARCAT

I am called by those that have seen my valour, Tearcat.

OMNES

Tearcat?

MOLL

A mere whip-jack, and that is, in the commonwealth of
rogues, a slave that can talk of sea-fight, name all your
chief pirates, discover more countries to you than either   125
the Dutch, Spanish, French, or English ever found out, yet
indeed all his service is by land, and that is to rob a fair, or
some such venturous exploit; Tearcat, foot sirrah, I have
your name, now I remember me, in my book of horners –
horns for the thumb, you know how.   130

TEARCAT

No indeed, Captain Moll (for I know you by sight), I am
no such nipping Christian, but a maunderer upon the
pad, I confess; and meeting with honest Trapdoor here,
whom you had cashiered from bearing arms, out at elbows

---

114 *the Isle of Dogs* the peninsula on the north bank of the Thames opposite
Greenwich: according to Sugden it took its name from hunting dogs being ken-
nelled there when Greenwich was a royal palace. It had become a place of refuge
for debtors and criminals; the name gave rise to frequent jokes of this kind. In
1598 the performance of a now lost play by Nashe and Jonson called *The Isle of
Dogs* led to the theatres being closed for two months. In *The Return from
Parnassus*, part 2, one of the students retires to the Isle of Dogs to become a professional satirist.

123 *whip-jack* a vagabond who pretends to be a distressed sailor: there is a similar description in Dekker's *Bellman of London*

130 *horns for the thumb* A horn-thumb was a thimble of horn used by cutpurses for
protecting the thumb against the edge of the knife used in cutting the purse-
strings; hence, by synecdoche, used of pickpockets themselves.

132 *nipping* thieving

132–3 *maunderer upon the pad* beggar on the highway; so *maunder* beg

under your colours, I instructed him in the rudiments of 135
roguery, and by my map made him sail over any country
you can name so that now he can maunder better than myself.

JACK DAPPER

So then, Trapdoor, thou art turned soldier now.

TRAPDOOR

Alas sir, now there's no wars, 'tis the safest course of life I 140
could take.

MOLL

I hope then you can cant, for by your cudgels, you, sirrah,
are an upright man.

TRAPDOOR

As any walks the highway, I assure you.

MOLL

And Tearcat, what are you? A wild rogue, an angler, or a 145
ruffler?

TEARCAT

Brother to this upright man, flesh and blood, ruffling
Tearcat is my name, and a ruffler is my style, my title, my
profession.

MOLL

Sirrah, where's your doxy? Halt not with me.   150

OMNES

Doxy, Moll, what's that?

MOLL

His wench.

TRAPDOOR

My doxy? I have by the solomon a doxy, that carries a
kinchin mort in her slate at her back, besides my dell and
my dainty wild dell, with all whom I'll tumble this next 155
darkmans in the strommel, and drink ben booze, and eat a
fat gruntling cheat, a cackling cheat, and a quacking cheat.

JACK DAPPER

Here's old cheating.

---

142 *you can cant* you have learnt all the appropriate specialist slang. For an expla-
     nation of the cant terms used in this scene, see the glossary given in the
     Appendix, and, generally, the various early authorities there cited.
150 *Halt not* don't limp, i.e. don't be roundabout or devious
154 *slate* See Appendix.
155–7 i.e. I'll tumble this next night in the straw, and drink good booze, and eat a
     fat pig, a capon, and a duck. For *booze* Q has *baufe*, which is evidently a misprint
     for *bouse* or *bowse*. See further in the Appendix.
158 *old* fine, rare

TRAPDOOR

My doxy stays for me in a boozing ken, brave captain.

MOLL

He says his wench stays for him in an alehouse: you are no   160
pure rogues.

TEARCAT

Pure rogues? No, we scorn to be pure rogues, but if you
come to our lib ken, or our stalling ken, you shall find
neither him nor me a queer cuffin.

MOLL

So sir, no churl of you?   165

TEARCAT

No, but a ben cove, a brave cove, a gentry cuffin.

LORD NOLAND

Call you this canting?

JACK DAPPER

Zounds, I'll give a schoolmaster half a crown a week, and
teach me this pedlar's French.

TRAPDOOR

Do but stroll, sir, half a harvest with us, sir, and you shall 170
gabble your bellyfull.

MOLL

Come you rogue, cant with me.

SIR THOMAS

Well said, Moll, cant with her, sirrah, and you shall have
money, else not a penny.

TRAPDOOR

I'll have a bout if she please.   175

MOLL

Come on sirrah.

TRAPDOOR

Ben mort, shall you and I heave a booth, mill a ken, or nip
a bung? And then we'll coach a hogshead under the ruffmans, and there you shall wap with me, and I'll niggle with
you.   180

MOLL

Out, you damned impudent rascal.

160–1 *you are no pure rogues* Bullen takes this to be ironical; but Moll may mean pure
in the sense of sexually pure or chaste, and that is certainly the sense in which
Tearcat picks up the word.

169 *pedlar's French* 'canting language to be found among none but beggars' (*Bellman
of London*); also applied generally to unintelligible jargon. Pedlars were widely
regarded as inescapably dishonest.

TRAPDOOR

Cut benar whids, and hold your fambles and your stamps.

LORD NOLAND

Nay, nay, Moll, why art thou angry? What was his gibber-
ish?

MOLL

Marry, this, my Lord, says he: Ben mort (good wench),   185
shall you and I heave a booth, mill a ken, or nip a bung?
Shall you and I rob a house, or cut a purse?

OMNES

Very good.

MOLL

And then we'll couch a hogshead under the ruffmans: and
then we'll lie under a hedge.   190

TRAPDOOR

That was my desire, captain, as 'tis fit a soldier should lie.

MOLL

And there you shall wap with me, and I'll niggle with you,
and that's all.

SIR BEAUTEOUS

Nay, nay, Moll, what's that wap?

JACK DAPPER

Nay teach me what niggling is, I'd fain be niggling.   195

MOLL

Wapping and niggling is all one, the rogue my man can tell
you.

TRAPDOOR

'Tis fadoodling, if it please you.

SIR BEAUTEOUS

This is excellent, one fit more, good Moll.

---

182 *Cut benar whids, and hold your fambles and your stamps* speak better words, and
hold your hands and your feet

198 *fadoodling OED* has nothing earlier than 1670 for 'fadoodle', when it meant
something ridiculous; but as Reed remarks, the explanation is evident from
Trapdoor's use of it.

199 *fit* strain or bout.

MOLL
Come you rogue, sing with me.   200

                    The song

              A gage of ben rom-booze
              In a boozing ken of Rom-ville
TEARCAT   Is benar than a caster,
              Peck, pennam, lap or popler,
              Which we mill in deuse a vill.   205
BOTH   Oh I would lib all the lightmans,
              Oh I would lib all the darkmans,
              By the solomon, under the ruffmans,
              By the solomon, in the hartmans.
TEARCAT   And scour the queer cramp-ring,   210
              And couch till a palliard docked my dell,
              So my boozy nab might skew rom-booze well.
BOTH   Avast to the pad, let us bing,
              Avast to the pad, let us bing.
OMNES
Fine knaves i'faith.   215
JACK DAPPER
The grating of ten new cartwheels, and the gruntling of

200–14 sp ed. In Q there is no speech prefix following Moll's invitation until the
third line of the song, where *T.Cat* is prefixed. At the sixth line *The song* appears
in the right-hand margin, where a chorus is strongly suggested. *T.Cat* is again
prefixed to the tenth line; the last two lines seem again to be a chorus. The song,
translated with the help of *Lanthorn and Candlelight*, means:
              A quart of good wine
              In an alehouse of London
              Is better than a cloak,
              Meat, bread, whey, or pottage,
              Which we steal in the country.
              Oh I would lie all the day,
              Oh I would lie all the night,
              By the mass, under the bushes,
              By the mass, in the stocks.
              And wear bolts (or fetters)
              And sleep till a tramp lay with my wench,
              So my boozy head might drink wine well.
              Away to the highway, let us go.
              Away to the highway, let us go.
    See Appendix for Dekker's definitions, and Moll's paraphrase at l. 241ff.
204 *lap* ed. (lay Q)
205 *vill* ed. (vile Q)
210 *cramp-ring* handcuffs, a cant adaptation of the standard word (cf. IV.ii.17–18
    and n.)

five hundred hogs coming from Romford market, cannot
make a worse noise than this canting language does in my
ears; pray, my Lord Noland, let's give these soldiers their
pay.   220

SIR BEAUTEOUS
Agreed, and let them march.

LORD NOLAND
Here, Moll.

MOLL
Now I see that you are stalled to the rogue, and are not
ashamed of your professions, look you: my Lord Noland
here and these gentlemen bestows upon you two, two   225
bordes and a half, that's two shillings sixpence.

TRAPDOOR
Thanks to your lordship.

TEARCAT
Thanks, heroical captain.

MOLL
Away.

TRAPDOOR
We shall cut ben whids of your masters and mistress-ship,   230
wheresoever we come.

MOLL
You'll maintain, sirrah, the old justice's plot to his face?

TRAPDOOR
Else trine me on the cheats: hang me.

MOLL
Be sure you meet me there.

TRAPDOOR
Without any more maundering I'll do't: follow, brave   235
Tearcat.

TEARCAT
I prae, sequor; let us go, mouse.

Exeunt they two, manet the rest

---

217 *Romford market* Romford had an important market, and allusions to Romford
hogs are frequent. Cf., e.g., *A Chaste Maid*, IV.i.98.

226 *bordes* shillings

230 *cut ben whids* speak well

233 *trine me on the cheats* hang me on the gallows; but cf. Appendix

235 *maundering* probably chattering; i.e. without more ado. The word is apparently
distinct from that used above at l. 132; but cf. Appendix.

237 *I prae, sequor* (Lat.) go before, I follow.
     sd *manet* (Lat.) remains

LORD NOLAND
    Moll, what was in that canting song?
MOLL
    Troth my Lord, only a praise of good drink, the only milk
    which these wild beasts love to suck, and thus it was: 240
        A rich cup of wine,
        Oh it is juice divine,
        More wholesome for the head
        Than meat, drink, or bread;
        To fill my drunken pate   245
        With that, I'd sit up late,
        By the heels would I lie,
        Under a lousy hedge die,
        Let a slave have a pull
        At my whore, so I be full   250
        Of that precious liquor
    – and a parcel of such stuff, my Lord, not worth the open-
    ing.

      Enter a CUTPURSE *very gallant, with four or five men after*
             him, one with a wand

LORD NOLAND
    What gallant comes yonder?
SIR THOMAS
    Mass, I think I know him, 'tis one of Cumberland.   255
1 CUTPURSE
    Shall we venture to shuffle in amongst yon heap of gallants
    and strike?
2 CUTPURSE
    'Tis a question whether there be any silver shells amongst
    them for all their satin outsides.
OMNES [CUTPURSES]
    Let's try.   260
MOLL
    Pox on him, a gallant? Shadow me, I know him: 'tis one
    that cumbers the land indeed; if he swim near to the shore
    of any of your pockets, look to your purses.
OMNES
    Is't possible?

253 sd *gallant* finely dressed
257 *strike* steal; to strike a hand is to do a job (*Lanthorn and Candlelight*, p. xxiv)
258 *shells* money
261 *Shadow me* follow me closely
264 sp OMNES i.e. Moll's companions

MOLL

   This brave fellow is no better than a foist.   265

OMNES

   Foist, what's that?

MOLL

   A diver with two fingers, a pickpocket; all his train study
the figging-law, that's to say cutting of purses and foisting;
one of them is a nip, I took him once i'the twopenny
gallery at the Fortune; then there's a cloyer, or snap, that   270
dogs any new brother in that trade, and snaps will have
half in any booty; he with the wand is both a stale, whose
office is to face a man i'the streets, whilst shells are drawn
by another, and then with his black conjuring rod in his
hand, he, by the nimbleness of his eye and juggling-stick,   275
will, in cheaping a piece of plate at a goldsmith's stall,
make four or five rings mount from the top of his
caduceus, and as if it were at leap-frog, they skip into his
hand presently.

2 CUTPURSE

   Zounds, we are smoked.   280

OMNES [CUTPURSES]

   Ha?

2 CUTPURSE

   We are boiled, pox on her; see, Moll, the roaring drab.

1 CUTPURSE

   All the diseases of sixteen hospitals boil her! Away.

MOLL

   Bless you, sir.

1 CUTPURSE

   And you, good sir.   285

MOLL

   Dost not ken me, man?

1 CUTPURSE

   No, trust me, sir.

265 *foist* etc. See Appendix.
269–70 *the twopenny gallery at the Fortune* not quite the cheapest place, for one could
    get in for a penny. The Fortune (see above, p. xxiii) was the theatre in which *The
    Roaring Girl* was then being performed.
276 *cheaping* bargaining for
278 *caduceus* strictly a herald's wand: I am not sure whether Moll is referring again
    to the cutpurse's stick used like a curb, or to a baton on which the goldsmith
    might keep rings for sale. Mercury, the nimble god of thieves, carried a ca-
    duceus; hence 'mercury': a dexterous thief.
287 *trust* ed. (rrust Q)

MOLL

Heart, there's a knight to whom I'm bound for many
favours lost his purse at the last new play i'the Swan, seven
angels in't: make it good, you're best; do you see? No   290
more.

1 CUTPURSE

A synagogue shall be called, Mistress Mary, disgrace me
not; pacus palabros, I will conjure for you, farewell.

                           [*Exeunt* CUTPURSES]

MOLL

Did not I tell you, my Lord?

LORD NOLAND

I wonder how thou camest to the knowledge of these nasty   295
villains.

SIR THOMAS

And why do the foul mouths of the world call thee Moll
Cutpurse? A name, methinks, damned and odious.

MOLL

Dare any step forth to my face and say,
'I have ta'en thee doing so, Moll'? I must confess,   300
In younger days, when I was apt to stray,
I have sat amongst such adders; seen their stings,
As any here might, and in full playhouses
Watched their quick-diving hands, to bring to shame
Such rogues, and in that stream met an ill name: 305
When next, my Lord, you spy any one of those,
So he be in his art a scholar, question him,
Tempt him with gold to open the large book
Of his close villainies: and you yourself shall cant
Better than poor Moll can, and know more laws   310
Of cheators, lifters, nips, foists, puggards, curbers,

288ff. This episode seems to be based on an established custom of Mary Frith's.
289 *Swan* the theatre on Bankside near the Globe
292 *synagogue* presumably an assembly of thieves to get the money together.
     Mulholland notes that Dekker refers to an underworld gathering as a 'satanical
     synagogue' in an allusion to Revelation 2, 9 in *Lanthorn and Candlelight*.
293 *pacus palabros* a corruption of Spanish *pocas palabras*, few words. Cf. *The Taming
     of the Shrew*, Ind. i.5
311 *cheators* or fingerers, those who win money by false dice: see Appendix
     lifters thieves (an old usage revived in 'shop-lifters')
     nips etc. See Appendix.
     puggards thieves: seemingly a unique occurrence, though cf. *The Winter's Tale*,
     IV.iii.7, for *pugging*. It is possible that we should read 'priggard', a word which
     in one form or another often occurs for thief.

With all the devil's black guard, than it is fit
Should be discovered to a noble wit.
I know they have their orders, offices,
Circuits and circles, unto which they are bound,   315
To raise their own damnation in.

JACK DAPPER   How dost thou know it?

MOLL

As you do, I show it you, they to me show it.
Suppose, my Lord, you were in Venice.

LORD NOLAND   Well.

MOLL

If some Italian pander there would tell
All the close tricks of courtesans, would not you   320
Hearken to such a fellow?

LORD NOLAND   Yes.

MOLL   And here,
Being come from Venice, to a friend most dear
That were to travel thither, you would proclaim
Your knowledge in those villainies, to save
Your friend from their quick danger: must you have   325
A black ill name, because ill things you know?
Good troth my Lord, I am made Moll Cutpurse so.
How many are whores in small ruffs and still looks!
How many chaste, whose names fill slander's books!
Were all men cuckolds, whom gallants in their scorns   330
Call so, we should not walk for goring horns.
Perhaps for my mad going some reprove me,
I please myself, and care not else who loves me.

OMNES

A brave mind, Moll, i'faith.

SIR THOMAS

Come my Lord, shall's to the ordinary?   335

LORD NOLAND

Ay, 'tis noon sure.

MOLL

Good my Lord, let not my name condemn me to you or to
the world: a fencer I hope may be called a coward, is he
so for that? If all that have ill names in London were to
be whipped, and to pay but twelve-pence apiece to the   340
beadle, I would rather have his office than a constable's.

---

312 *black guard* a guard of attendants, black in person, dress, or character: cf.
    Lanthorn and Candlelight, p. ii: 'The great Lord of Limbo did therefore com-
    mand all his Black Guard ... to bestir them'
316 *raise ... in* make more complete (literally to fatten)
325 *quick* lively

JACK DAPPER
  So would I, Captain Moll: 'twere a sweet tickling office
  i'faith.   *Exeunt*

[Act V, Scene ii]

Enter SIR ALEXANDER WENGRAVE, GOSHAWK *and*
GREENWIT, *and others*

SIR ALEXANDER
  My son marry a thief, that impudent girl,
  Whom all the world stick their worst eyes upon?
GREENWIT
  How will your care prevent it?
GOSHAWK   'Tis impossible.
  They marry close, they're gone, but none knows whither.
SIR ALEXANDER
  Oh gentlemen, when has a father's heart-strings   5
  Held out so long from breaking?

                    Enter a SERVANT

                              Now what news, sir?
SERVANT
  They were met upo'th'water an hour since, sir,
  Putting in towards the Sluice.
SIR ALEXANDER   The Sluice? Come gentlemen,

                              [*Exit* SERVANT]

  'Tis Lambeth works against us.
GREENWIT   And that Lambeth
  Joins more mad matches than your six wet towns,   10

---

342 *tickling* diverting, but 'tickler' was also slang for a whip

  4 *close* secretly
  8 *the Sluice* The Sluice was an embankment built to protect the low-lying area of
    Lambeth Marsh from inundations; it was used as a landing-place. Perhaps we
    are meant also to think of the verb to sluice (= to copulate with).
  9 *Lambeth* was also renowned as the haunt of thieves, etc.; but there is perhaps an
    allusion to the boat-building works there; additionally Lambeth was the place
    from which (after crossing the river by boat) one would set out towards the
    south-west.
 10 *your six wet* (i.e. riverside) *towns* A note in Reed's edition of Dodsley suggests
    that the six are Fulham, Richmond, Kingston, Hampton, Chertsey, and Staines.

'Twixt that and Windsor Bridge, where fares lie soaking.
SIR ALEXANDER
Delay no time, sweet gentlemen: to Blackfriars,
We'll take a pair of oars and make after 'em.

Enter TRAPDOOR

TRAPDOOR
Your son, and that bold masculine ramp
My mistress, are landed now at Tower.
SIR ALEXANDER   Hoyda, at Tower?   15
TRAPDOOR
I heard it now reported.   [*Exit*]
SIR ALEXANDER   Which way, gentlemen,
Shall I bestow my care? I'm drawn in pieces
Betwixt deceit and shame.

Enter SIR [GUY] FITZ-ALLARD

SIR GUY   Sir Alexander,
You're well met, and most rightly served:
My daughter was a scorn to you.
SIR ALEXANDER   Say not so, sir.   20
SIR GUY
A very abject she, poor gentlewoman.
Your house has been dishonoured: give you joy, sir,
Of your son's gaskin-bride, you'll be a grandfather shortly
To a fine crew of roaring sons and daughters,
'Twill help to stock the suburbs passing well, sir.   25

---

11 *where fares lie soaking* In more recent centuries, to 'soak' can mean to linger over sexual intercourse; and the whole phrase suggests the use of the riverside towns for sexual excursions.
12 *to Blackfriars* i.e. they will take a boat from Blackfriars Stairs and cross to Lambeth
14 *ramp* Cf. III.iii.7.
21 *abject* here, a noun meaning 'outcast'
22 *has* ed. (had Q)
23 *gaskin-bride* one, that is, wearing gaskins or loose breeches: the Q spelling is Gaskoyne, which indicates a popular and possibly correct etymology (i.e. from Gascony)
25 *the suburbs* were notoriously corrupt, licentious, and full of brothels. Cf. Nashe, *Christ's Tears over Jerusalem* (Works [1904], II, 148): 'London, what are thy suburbs but licensed stews?' But those living in the suburbs would be penniless too: cf. *Lanthorn and Candlelight*, p. ix: 'these suburb sinners have no land to live upon but their legs'. A suburb-sinner was a prostitute. And see the Prologus to this play, l. 21.

SIR ALEXANDER
　　Oh play not with the miseries of my heart.
　　Wounds should be dressed and healed, not vexed, or left
　　Wide open, to the anguish of the patient,
　　And scornful air let in: rather let pity
　　And advice charitably help to refresh 'em.　　　　　　　30
SIR GUY
　　Who'd place his charity so unworthily,
　　Like one that gives alms to a cursing beggar?
　　Had I but found one spark of goodness in you
　　Toward my deserving child, which then grew fond
　　Of your son's virtues, I had eased you now.　　　　　　35
　　But I perceive both fire of youth and goodness
　　Are raked up in the ashes of your age,
　　Else no such shame should have come near your house,
　　Nor such ignoble sorrow touch your heart.
SIR ALEXANDER
　　If not for worth, for pity's sake assist me.　　　　　　40
GREENWIT
　　You urge a thing past sense, how can he help you?
　　All his assistance is as frail as ours,
　　Full as uncertain where's the place that holds 'em.
　　One brings us water-news; then comes another
　　With a full-charged mouth, like a culverin's voice,　　45
　　And he reports the Tower: whose sounds are truest?
GOSHAWK
　　In vain you flatter him, Sir Alexander.
SIR ALEXANDER
　　I flatter him? Gentlemen, you wrong me grossly.
GREENWIT
　　He does it well i'faith.
SIR GUY　　　　　　　　　Both news are false,
　　Of Tower or water: they took no such way yet.　　　　50

---

37 *raked up* smothered
45 *culverin* a large cannon
48 sp SIR ALEXANDER ed. (Fitz-All. Q) I take it that Goshawk means flatter in the
　　sense of coax or wheedle, but Sir Alexander mistakes this for the common use.
　　If Q is correct, presumably Goshawk is being ironic: one must then, with pre-
　　vious editors, punctuate his speech '. . . flatter him. Sir Alexander –', as if he were
　　going to explain why 'flattery' will get him nowhere; but there seems no reason
　　why such a speech should come at this point.
49 Does this mean that Goshawk and Greenwit are in the Fitz-Allard plot? Cf.
　　l. 92.

SIR ALEXANDER
  Oh strange: hear you this, gentlemen, yet more plunges?
SIR GUY
  They're nearer than you think for, yet more close
  Than if they were further off.
SIR ALEXANDER   How am I lost
  In these distractions?
SIR GUY   For your speeches, gentlemen,
  In taxing me for rashness, 'fore you all   55
  I will engage my state to half his wealth,
  Nay to his son's revenues, which are less,
  And yet nothing at all till they come from him,
  That I could (if my will stuck to my power)
  Prevent this marriage yet, nay banish her   60
  Forever from his thoughts, much more his arms.
SIR ALEXANDER
  Slack not this goodness, though you heap upon me
  Mountains of malice and revenge hereafter:
  I'd willingly resign up half my state to him,
  So he would marry the meanest drudge I hire.   65
GREENWIT
  He talks impossibilities, and you believe 'em.
SIR GUY
  I talk no more than I know how to finish,
  My fortunes else are his that dares stake with me.
  The poor young gentleman I love and pity,
  And to keep shame from him (because the spring   70
  Of his affection was my daughter's first,
  Till his frown blasted all), do but estate him
  In those possessions which your love and care
  Once pointed out for him, that he may have room
  To entertain fortunes of noble birth,   75
  Where now his desperate wants casts him upon her:
  And if I do not, for his own sake chiefly,

51 *plunges* dilemmas; cf. IV.i.152
52 *think for* suppose
   close secret, hidden
54–5 'Though I foresee that you will tax me with rashness.'
56 *engage* wager
   his i.e. Sir Alexander's
59 *if my will stuck to my power* if I would do what I could
70–1 'Because the fountain of his love belonged first to my daughter'
72 *his* i.e. Sir Alexander's
76 *her* i.e. Moll

Rid him of this disease that now grows on him,
I'll forfeit my whole state, before these gentlemen.
GREENWIT
    Troth but you shall not undertake such matches,   80
    We'll persuade so much with you.
SIR ALEXANDER   Here's my ring,
He will believe this token: 'fore these gentlemen
I will confirm it fully: all those lands
My first love 'lotted him, he shall straight possess
In that refusal.
SIR GUY   If I change it not,   85
    Change me into a beggar.
GREENWIT   Are you mad, sir?
SIR GUY
    'Tis done.
GOSHAWK   Will you undo yourself by doing,
And show a prodigal trick in your old days?
SIR ALEXANDER
    'Tis a match, gentlemen.
SIR GUY   Ay, ay, sir, ay.
I ask no favour; trust to you for none,   90
My hope rests in the goodness of your son.   *Exit*
GREENWIT
    He holds it up well yet.
GOSHAWK   Of an old knight i'faith.
SIR ALEXANDER
    Cursed be the time I laid his first love barren,
Wilfully barren, that before this hour
Had sprung forth fruits of comfort and of honour;   95
He loved a virtuous gentlewoman.

Enter MOLL [*in male dress*]

GOSHAWK   Life,
    Here's Moll.
GREENWIT   Jack?
GOSHAWK   How dost thou, Jack?
MOLL   How dost thou, gallant?
SIR ALEXANDER
    Impudence, where's my son?
MOLL   Weakness, go look him.

80 *matches* wagers
85 *In that refusal* i.e. in refusing Moll
92 *Of* in the true manner of

SIR ALEXANDER
    Is this your wedding gown?
MOLL   The man talks monthly:
    Hot broth and a dark chamber for the knight,   100
    I see he'll be stark mad at our next meeting.   *Exit*
GOSHAWK
    Why sir, take comfort now, there's no such matter.
    No priest will marry her, sir, for a woman
    Whiles that shape's on, and it was never known
    Two men were married and conjoined in one: 105
    Your son hath made some shift to love another.
SIR ALEXANDER
    Whate'er she be, she has my blessing with her,
    May they be rich, and fruitful, and receive
    Like comfort to their issue as I take
    In them. Has pleased me now: marrying not this,   110
    Through a whole world he could not choose amiss.
GREENWIT
    Glad y'are so penitent for your former sin, sir.
GOSHAWK
    Say he should take a wench with her smock-dowry,
    No portion with her but her lips and arms?
SIR ALEXANDER
    Why, who thrive better, sir? They have most blessing,   115
    Though other have more wealth, and least repent:
    Many that want most know the most content.
GREENWIT
    Say he should marry a kind youthful sinner?

---

99 *The man talks monthly* i.e. madly (as if under the influence of the moon). Cf.
    Lanthorn and Candlelight, viii: 'A moon-man signifies in English a "madman" be-
    cause the moon hath greatest domination above any other planet over the bod-
    ies of frantic persons.'
100 *Hot broth and a dark chamber* treatments for insanity. The darkness was to rest
    the overstimulated imagination.
103 *No priest will marry her ... for a woman* 'Marriages' between two men crop up in
    several plays, e.g. Fletcher's *Wild Goose Chase* and *Monsieur Thomas*.
113 *with her smock-dowry* i.e. with no dowry but her smock: apparently a unique oc-
    currence, but cf. *A Chaste Maid*, III.iii.77: 'I took her with one smock', and *A
    Trick to Catch the Old One*, IV.iv.8: 'She's worth four hundred a year in her very
    smock.'
118 *kind* winsome

SIR ALEXANDER
  Age will quench that,
  Any offence but theft and drunkenness,   120
  Nothing but death can wipe away:
  Their sins are green even when their heads are grey.
  Nay I despair not now, my heart's cheered, gentlemen,
  No face can come unfortunately to me.

                    Enter a SERVANT

  Now, sir, your news?
SERVANT   Your son with his fair bride   125
  Is near at hand.
SIR ALEXANDER   Fair may their fortunes be.
GREENWIT
  Now you're resolved, sir, it was never she?
SIR ALEXANDER
  I find it in the music of my heart.

            Enter MOLL *masked, in* SEBASTIAN'*s hand, and*
                         FITZ-ALLARD

  See where they come.
GOSHAWK   A proper lusty presence, sir.
SIR ALEXANDER
  Now has he pleased me right, I always counselled him   130
  To choose a goodly personable creature,
  Just of her pitch was my first wife his mother.
SEBASTIAN
  Before I dare discover my offence,
  I kneel for pardon.
SIR ALEXANDER   My heart gave it thee
  Before thy tongue could ask it: 135
  Rise, thou hast raised my joy to greater height
  Than to that seat where grief dejected it:
  Both welcome to my love and care for ever.
  Hide not my happiness too long, all's pardoned,
  Here are our friends, salute her, gentlemen.   140

                    They unmask her

119–21 *stet* Q (except for lineation, Q making a single line from *Age* to *drunkenness*).
    The sense is obscure as the sentence stands, and faulty lineation suggests that
    there may be corruption. Possibly we should read (l. 121) 'And these nothing
    but death can wipe away' – or some such phrase.
127 *resolved* persuaded
132 *pitch* height

OMNES
    Heart, who's this? Moll!
SIR ALEXANDER
    Oh my reviving shame, is't I must live
    To be struck blind? Be it the work of sorrow,
    Before age take't in hand.
SIR GUY   Darkness and death.
    Have you deceived me thus? Did I engage   145
    My whole estate for this?
SIR ALEXANDER   You asked no favour,
    And you shall find as little; since my comforts
    Play false with me, I'll be as cruel to thee
    As grief to fathers' hearts.
MOLL   Why, what's the matter with you,
    'Less too much joy should make your age forgetful?   150
    Are you too well, too happy?
SIR ALEXANDER   With a vengeance.
MOLL
    Methinks you should be proud of such a daughter,
    As good a man as your son.
SIR ALEXANDER   Oh monstrous impudence.
MOLL
    You had no note before, an unmarked knight;
    Now all the town will take regard on you,   155
    And all your enemies fear you for my sake:
    You may pass where you list, through crowds most thick,
    And come off bravely with your purse unpicked.
    You do not know the benefits I bring with me:
    No cheat dares work upon you with thumb or knife,   160
    While y'ave a roaring girl to your son's wife.
SIR ALEXANDER
    A devil rampant.
SIR GUY   Have you so much charity
    Yet to release me of my last rash bargain,
    And I'll give in your pledge?
SIR ALEXANDER   No sir, I stand to't,
    I'll work upon advantage, as all mischiefs   165

---

141 *who's this? Moll!* ed. (who this *Mol*? Q)
150 *'Less* unless
154 *unmarked* unnoticed, of no account
160 *cheat* in the general sense of pickpocket or cutpurse
    thumb Cf. V.i.130 and n.
165 *work upon advantage* take advantage of my position (unscrupulously): cf. *A Fair
    Quarrel*, III.iii.151

Do upon me.
SIR GUY   Content: bear witness all then,
His are the lands, and so contention ends.
Here comes your son's bride, 'twixt two noble friends.

Enter the LORD NOLAND *and* SIR BEAUTEOUS GANYMEDE
with MARY FITZ-ALLARD *between them, the* CITIZENS *and
their* WIVES *with them*

MOLL
Now are you gulled as you would be: thank me for't,
I'd a forefinger in't.
SEBASTIAN   Forgive me, father: 170
Though there before your eyes my sorrow feigned,
This still was she for whom true love complained.
SIR ALEXANDER
Blessings eternal and the joys of angels
Begin your peace here, to be signed in heaven!
How short my sleep of sorrow seems now to me,   175
To this eternity of boundless comforts,
That finds no want but utterance and expression.
My Lord, your office here appears so honourably,
So full of ancient goodness, grace, and worthiness,
I never took more joy in sight of man   180
Than in your comfortable presence now.
LORD NOLAND
Nor I more delight in doing grace to virtue,
Than in this worthy gentlewoman, your son's bride,
Noble Fitz-Allard's daughter, to whose honour
And modest fame I am a servant vowed,   185
So is this knight.
SIR ALEXANDER   Your loves make my joys proud.
Bring forth those deeds of land my care laid ready,
And which, old knight, thy nobleness may challenge,
Joined with thy daughter's virtues, whom I prize now
As dearly as that flesh I call mine own.   190
Forgive me, worthy gentlewoman, 'twas my blindness
When I rejected thee; I saw thee not,
Sorrow and wilful rashness grew like films
Over the eyes of judgment, now so clear
I see the brightness of thy worth appear.   195
MARY
Duty and love may I deserve in those,

188 *challenge* claim
196 *those* i.e. the eyes of judgment

And all my wishes have a perfect close.
SIR ALEXANDER
    That tongue can never err, the sound's so sweet.
    Here, honest son, receive into thy hands
    The keys of wealth, possession of those lands   200
    Which my first care provided, they're thine own:
    Heaven give thee a blessing with 'em; the best joys
    That can in worldly shapes to man betide
    Are fertile lands and a fair fruitful bride,
    Of which I hope thou'rt sped.
SEBASTIAN   I hope so too sir.   205
MOLL
    Father and son, I ha' done you simple service here.
SEBASTIAN
    For which thou shalt not part, Moll, unrequited.
SIR ALEXANDER
    Thou art a mad girl, and yet I cannot now
    Condemn thee.
MOLL   Condemn me? Troth and you should, sir,
    I'd make you seek out one to hang in my room,   210
    I'd give you the slip at gallows, and cozen the people.
    Heard you this jest, my Lord?
LORD NOLAND   What is it, Jack?
MOLL
    He was in fear his son would marry me,
    But never dreamt that I would ne'er agree.
LORD NOLAND
    Why? Thou hadst a suitor once, Jack, when wilt marry?   215
MOLL
    Who, I, my Lord? I'll tell you when i'faith:
                When you shall hear
                Gallants void from sergeants' fear,
                Honesty and truth unslandered,
                Woman manned but never pandered,   220
                Cheats booted but not coached,
                Vessels older ere they're broached.
                If my mind be then not varied,
                Next day following I'll be married.

205 *sped* provided; but (cf. previous line) to speed is to be sexually potent
206 *simple* pure, disinterested
209 *and* if
221 *not coached* so unsuccessful in their cheating that they cannot afford to travel by
    coach
222 *Vessels* i.e. maidenheads

LORD NOLAND
    This sounds like doomsday.
MOLL   Then were marriage best,   225
    For if I should repent, I were soon at rest.
SIR ALEXANDER
    In troth thou'rt a good wench, I'm sorry now
    The opinion was so hard I conceived of thee.
    Some wrongs I've done thee.

                    Enter TRAPDOOR

TRAPDOOR   Is the wind there now?
    'Tis time for me to kneel and confess first,   230
    For fear it come too late and my brains feel it.
    Upon my paws I ask you pardon, mistress.
MOLL
    Pardon? For what, sir? What has your rogueship done
    now?
TRAPDOOR
    I have been from time to time hired to confound you   235
    By this old gentleman.
MOLL   How?
TRAPDOOR   Pray forgive him,
    But may I counsel you, you should never do't.
    Many a snare to entrap your worship's life
    Have I laid privily, chains, watches, jewels,
    And when he saw nothing could mount you up,   240
    Four hollow-hearted angels he then gave you,
    By which he meant to trap you, I to save you.
SIR ALEXANDER
    To all which shame and grief in me cry guilty:
    Forgive me, now I cast the world's eyes from me,
    And look upon thee freely with mine own,   245
    I see the most of many wrongs before thee
    Cast from the jaws of envy and her people,
    And nothing foul but that. I'll never more
    Condemn by common voice, for that's the whore
    That deceives man's opinion, mocks his trust,   250
    Cozens his love, and makes his heart unjust.
MOLL
    Here be the angels, gentlemen, they were given me

237 *may I counsel you* if you take my advice
241 *hollow-hearted angels* i.e. with holes through the middle; cf. IV.i.200
246 *thee* ed. (hee Q)   *before thee* done to thee
247 *Cast* i.e. are cast, thrown at you

As a musician. I pursue no pity:
Follow the law: and you can cuck me, spare not:
Hang up my viol by me, and I care not.   255
SIR ALEXANDER
So far I'm sorry, I'll thrice double 'em
To make thy wrongs amends.
Come, worthy friends, my honourable Lord,
Sir Beauteous Ganymede, and noble Fitz-Allard,
And you kind gentlewomen, whose sparkling presence   260
Are glories set in marriage, beams of society,
For all your loves give lustre to my joys:
The happiness of this day shall be remembered
At the return of every smiling spring:
In my time now 'tis born, and may no sadness   265
Sit on the brows of men upon that day,
But as I am so all go pleased away.   [*Exeunt*]

EPILOGUS

A painter having drawn with curious art
The picture of a woman (every part
Limned to the life) hung out the piece to sell:
People who passed along, viewing it well,
Gave several verdicts on it: some dispraised   5
The hair, some said the brows too high were raised,
Some hit her o'er the lips, misliked their colour,
Some wished her nose were shorter, some the eyes fuller;
Others said roses on her cheeks should grow,
Swearing they looked too pale, others cried no.   10
The workman, still as fault was found, did mend it
In hope to please all; but, this work being ended
And hung open at stall, it was so vile,
So monstrous and so ugly all men did smile

253 *pursue* seek
254 *and you can cuck me* if you can get me into a cucking stool
260 *gentlewomen* ed. (gentlewoman Q): addressed to the citizens' wives; *Are* in the
    following line is influenced by this plural
261 *beams* sunbeams
265 *In my time* Bowers amends to 'May time'; but Q is perfectly intelligible – Sir
    Alexander hopes the happiness will be remembered beyond his own time.

Epilogus   Probably delivered by Moll
  7 *hit ... o'er* directed their criticism toward
 11 *still as* each time

At the poor painter's folly. Such we doubt   15
Is this our comedy: some perhaps do flout
The plot, saying 'tis too thin, too weak, too mean;
Some for the person will revile the scene,
And wonder that a creature of her being
Should be the subject of a poet, seeing   20
In the world's eye none weighs so light: others look
For all those base tricks published in a book
(Foul as his brains they flowed from) of cutpurses,
Of nips and foists, nasty, obscene discourses,
As full of lies, as empty of worth or wit,   25
For any honest ear, or eye, unfit. And thus,
If we to every brain that's humorous
Should fashion scenes, we (with the painter) shall
In striving to please all, please none at all.
Yet for such faults, as either the writers' wit   30
Or negligence of the actors do commit,
Both crave your pardons: if what both have done
Cannot full pay your expectation,
The Roaring Girl herself, some few days hence,
Shall on this stage give larger recompense.   35
Which mirth that you may share in, herself does woo you,
And craves this sign, your hands to beckon her to you.

                          FINIS

22 *a book* See above, p. xix.
23 *cutpurses* ed. (cutpurse Q)
27 *humorous* whimsical, full of humours or fancies
34–5 There has been much discussion about what these lines refer to (see above,
p. xviii). Though the assumption has been commonly made that Mary Frith herself is the subject of them, it is possible that the allusion is to the actor playing
the part, who presumably would shortly act again in another comedy on the
same stage. See Mulholland, 'The Date of *The Roaring Girl*', *RES,* new series 28
(1977), 19–20.

APPENDIX

Cant and Canting

> This word *canting* seems to be derived from the Latin verb
> *canto*, which signifies in English 'to sing' or 'to make a sound
> with words', that's to say 'to speak'. And very aptly may *cant-*
> *ing* take his derivation *a cantando* 'from singing' because
> amongst these beggarly consorts, that can play upon no better
> instruments, the language of *canting* is a kind of music and he
> that in such assemblies can *cant* best is counted the best mu-
> sician. (Dekker, *English Villainies Discovered by Lanthorn and*
> *Candlelight*, p.i).

Dekker got most of his knowledge of underworld cant at second
hand. His three tracts on roguery – *The Seven Deadly Sins of London*
(1606), *The Bellman of London*, and *Lanthorn and Candlelight* (both
1608) – were latecomers in a tradition of 'manifest detections'
which began perhaps with Robert Copland's *Highway to the Spital-*
house (1535) and has its more modern derivatives in extensive
dictionaries of cant and slang. Dekker depended heavily on his pre-
decessors, in particular on Thomas Harman's *A Caveat for Common*
Cursitors (1566), a book which, according to S. R. (probably
Samuel Rid), the somewhat peppery author of *Martin Mark-All*
(1610), was out of date and inaccurate by the early seventeenth
century. The third edition of *Lanthorn and Candlelight* (1612) con-
sequently included a supplement called 'O per se O' – probably,
but not certainly, by Dekker – expanding and occasionally silently
correcting earlier information. Most of these tracts contain brief
'canter's dictionaries', which by and large confirm one another's
definitions: the following glossary of cant words in *The Roaring Girl*
is compiled, wherever possible, from Dekker's, with substantive
variants noted from other sources. The sigla used are as follows:

- B: *The Bellman of London* (Dekker, 1608)
- C: *A Caveat for Common Cursitors* (Thomas Harman, 1566)
- F: *The Fraternity of Vagabonds* (John Awdeley, 1561)
- L: *Lanthorn and Candlelight* (Dekker, 1608)
- M: *Martin Mark-All, Beadle of Bridewell* (Stationers' Register, 1610)
- N: *A Notable Discovery of Cozenage* (Robert Greene, 1591)
- O: *O per se O* (Dekker?, 1612)

Angler: 'a limb of an upright-man ... in the day time, they beg from house to house, not so much for relief, as to spy what lies fit for their nets, which in the night following they fish for. The rod they angle with is a staff of five or six foot in length, in which within one inch of the top is a little hole bored quite through, into which hole they put an iron hook, and with the same do they angle at windows about midnight, the draught they pluck up being apparel, sheets, coverlets, or whatsoever their iron hooks can lay hold of' (B)

Ben, benar: good, better (L)

Ben cove: see under *Cove*

Bing: come, go (L)

Bing awast (or *avast*): get you hence (L); steal away (O)

Boil: see under *Smoke*

Booze (or *bouse*): drink (L)

Boozing ken: alehouse (L, O)

Borde: shilling (L)

Bung: purse (L); 'now used for a pocket, heretofore for a purse' (M)

Cackling cheat: cock or capon: see *Cheat*

Caster: cloak (L)

Cheat: thing. 'By joining of two simples do they make almost all their compounds. As for example, *nab* in the canting tongue is a head, and *nab cheat* is a hat or a cap. Which word *cheat*, being coupled to other words, stands in very good stead and does excellent service ... a *muffling cheat* signifies a napkin, a *belly cheat* an apron, a *grunting cheat* a pig, a *cackling cheat* a cock or capon, a *quacking cheat* a duck ... and so may that word be married to many others besides' (L). The word is of course also used in the play in its standard sense.

Cheator: 'The Cheating Law, or the art of winning money by false dice: those that practise this study call themselves *cheators*, the dice *cheaters*, and the money which they purchase *cheats*' (B). For a more detailed explanation, see F.

Cheats (*chats, chates*): the gallows (L, C). 'Here he [the Bellman] mistakes both the simple word, because he found it so printed, not knowing the true original thereof, and also in the compound. As for *chates* it should be *cheats*, which word is used generally for things ... so that if you will make a word for gallows, you must put thereto this word, *trining*, which signifies hanging; and so *trining-cheat* is as much as to say "hanging-things", or the gallows, and not *chates*' (M).

Cloyer: see under *Figging-Law*; '*priggers, filchers* and *cloyers* (being all in English stealers)' (O)

Couch a hogshead: lie down asleep (L). 'This phrase is like an almanac that is out of date: now the Dutch word *slope* is with them used, "to sleep", and *liggen*, "to lie down"' (M).

Cove, Cuffin: 'The word *cove* or *cofe* or *cuffin* signifies a man, a fellow, etc., but differs something in his property according as it meets with other words, for a gentleman is called a *gentry cove* or *cofe*, a good fellow is a *ben cofe*, a churl is called a *queer cuffin* (*queer* signifies naught and *cuffin*, as I said before, a man) and in canting they term a Justice of the Peace (because he punisheth them, belike) by no other name than by *queer cuffin*, that's to say a churl or a naughty man' (L).

Cramp-ring: hand-cuff; and see under *Scour*

Curber: 'The Curbing Law [teaches] how to hook goods out of a window ... He that hooks is called the *curber* ... The hook is the *curb*' (B) cf. *Angler.*

Cut ben (benar) whids: speak good (better) words (L); tell the truth (M)

Darkmans: the night (L)

Dell: 'A dell is a young wench ... but as yet not spoiled of her maidenhead ["able for generation, and not yet known or broken" (C)]. These dells are reserved as dishes for the upright-men, for none but they must have the first taste of them' (B)

Deuse a vill (or *deuceville*)*:* the country (L)

Dock: lie with, copulate, by analogy with a ship coming into dock

Doxy: whore (O); 'his woman ... which he calleth his altham, if she be his wife, and if she be his harlot, she is called his doxy' (F); 'these doxies be broken and spoiled of their maidenhead by the upright-men, and then they have their name of doxies, and not afore' (C)

Fadoodling: copulating; a fadoodle is 'something foolish' (*OED*), so fadoodling is 'playing around'

Fambles: hands (L)

Figging-Law: 'Cutting of purses and picking of pockets' (N): 'In making of which law, two persons have the chief voices, that is to say, the cutpurse and the pickpocket, and all the branches of this law reach to none but them and such as are made free denizens of their incorporation ... He that cuts the purse is called the *nip*, he that is half with him is the *snap* or the *cloyer* ... He that picks the pocket is called a *foist*, he that faceth the man is the *stale*' (B).

Foist: see under *Figging-Law*

Gage: a quart pot (L)

Gentry cuffin: see under *Cove*

Ging: company, gang (Dekker, *Penny-Wise, Pound-Foolish*)

Glaziers: eyes (L)

Goll: hand (Dekker, *The Wonderful Year*)

Grunt(l)ing cheat: pig; see *Cheat*

Hartmans (or *harmans*)*:* the stocks (L)

Heave a booth (or *bough*)*:* rob a booth (L)

Ken: house (L)

Kinchin mort: 'Kinchin-morts are girls of a year or two old, which the *morts* (their mothers) carry at their backs in their slates (which in the canting-tongue are sheets)' (B).

Lap: buttermilk or whey (L)

Lib: sleep (L)

Libken: a house to lie in (L); a house to lodge people (M)

Lifter: 'The Lifting Law ... teacheth a kind of lifting of goods clean away' (B).

Lightmans: the day

Maund: to ask (F, L); to beg (M, O)

Maunder, maunderer: beggar (O)

Mill: to steal or rob (L)

Mort: woman (esp. one who has fallen from a better state) (L)

Mutton: food for lust (*OED*), hence a prostitute

Nab: head (L)

Niggle: to company with a woman (L). 'This word is not now used, but *wapping*, and thereof comes the name *wapping-morts*, whores' (M).

Nip (noun): see under *Figging-Law*

Nip a bung: to cut a purse (L)

Pad: a way, highway (L)

Palliard: 'he that goeth in a patched cloak' (F); some are 'natural' (born to the trade), some 'artificial': the latter 'carrieth about him the great *cleyme* [an artificially induced sore] to stir compassion up in people's hearts' (O)

Pannun (pannam or *pennam):* bread (L)

Peck: meat (L). '*Peck* is not meat, but *peckage*. *Peck* is taken to eat or bite' (M).

Pedlar's French: 'that canting language which is to be found among none but beggars' (B), 'invented to th'intent that, albeit any spies should secretly steal into their companies to discover them, they might freely utter their minds one to another, yet avoid that danger' (L)

Poplars (or *popler*): porridge (C), pottage (L)

Priggard (prigger or *prigman):* a stealer generally (O), but applied especially to *priggers of prancers* (horse-thieves) (N). But 'a prigman goeth with a stick ... to steal clothes off the hedge' (F).

Quacking-cheat: duck; see under *Cheat*

Queer: naught, naughty (L)

Queer cuffin: see under *Cove*

Rom-booze (or *rom-bouse):* wine (L). 'This word [*rom* or *room*] is always taken in the best sense, to show a thing extraordinary or excellent' (M).

Rom-ville: London (L), or more generally a great town (M)

Ruffler: 'a ruffler goeth with a weapon to seek service, saying he hath been a servitor in the wars, and beggeth for his relief' (F). 'The ruffler and the upright-man are so like in conditions, that you would swear them brothers: they walk with cudgels alike; they profess arms alike ... These commonly are fellows that have stood aloof in the wars, and whilst others fought, they took their heels and ran away from their captain, or else they would have been serving-men, whom for their behaviour no man would trust with a livery' (B).

Ruffmans: hedges, woods, or bushes (L). 'Not the hedge or bushes as heretofore; but now the eavesing of houses or roofs. *Cragmans* is now used for the hedge' (M).

Solomon: the Mass (L), used chiefly in oaths

Scour the (queer) cramp-ring: to wear bolts or fetters (C)

Shells: money (B)

Shifter: cozener (F)

Skelder: to live by begging, especially by passing oneself off as a wounded or disbanded soldier

Skew: all authorities agree that this means a cup (C, L, M); but in *The Roaring Girl* it is used as a verb, meaning to drink

Slate: sheet; see under *Kinchin mort*

Smoke: 'The spying of this villainy is called smoking or boiling' (B).

Snap: 'he that is half with him [the nip]' (N): see under *Figging-Law* and *Upright-man*

Stale: see under *Figging-Law*

Stall: to make or ordain (L)

Stalled to the rogue: 'I do stall thee to the rogue by virtue of this sovereign English liquor, so that henceforth it shall be lawful for thee to cant, that is to say to be a vagabond and to beg' (B).

Stalling- (or *stuling-*) *ken:* house for receiving stolen goods (L)

Stamps: legs (L)

Strike: 'the act doing' (in figging-law) (N)

Strommel (or *strummel*): straw (L)

Synagogue: an assembly of thieves (?)

Trine: hang (L); see also under *Cheats*

Upright-man: 'a sturdy big-boned knave, that never walks but (like a commander) with a short truncheon in his hand, which he calls his filchman. At markets, fairs, and other meetings his voice among beggars is of the same sound that a constable's is of, it is not to be controlled' (B). 'This man is of so much authority that, meeting with any of his profession, he may call them to account, and command a share or snap unto himself of all that they have gained by their trade in one month' (F).

Wap: see under *Niggle*

Whip-jack: 'Another sort of knaves ... are called whip-jacks, who talk of nothing but fights at sea, piracies, drownings and shipwrecks' (B). 'These fresh-water mariners, their ships were drowned in the plain of Salisbury' (C).

Wild dell: a dell born to the position: 'those such as are born or begotten under a hedge' (B)

Wild rogue: 'one that is born a rogue ... begotten in barn or bushes, and from his infancy traded up in treachery'; 'a rogue is neither so stout or hardy as the upright-man' (C). He 'is a spirit that cares not in what circle he rises, nor into the company of what devils he falls: in his swaddling clouts is he marked to be a villain, and in his breeding is instructed to be so ... These wild rogues (like wild geese) keep in flocks, and all the day loiter in fields, if the weather be warm, and at brick-kilns, or else disperse themselves in cold weather, to rich men's doors, and at night have their meetings in barns or other out-places' (B).

A selection of these various tracts (not all printed complete) was compiled by A. V. Judges and published in 1930 as *The Elizabethan Underworld*; some have been reprinted by the Early English Text Society (1869) and the New Shakespeare Society (1880). Dekker's (without *O per se O*) were included in Grosart's edition of the non-dramatic works (1884–6) and in an edition by O. Smeaton (1904). *Lanthorn and Candlelight* is reprinted complete, with *O per se O*, in a collection of Dekker's tales and tracts edited by E. D. Pendry (1967).